Peter Gibson

Shakespeare's Second Globe

THE MISSING MONUMENT

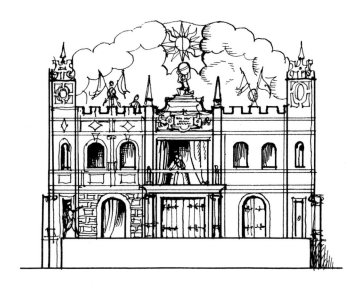

C. WALTER HODGES

Shakespeare's Second Globe

THE MISSING MONUMENT

OXFORD UNIVERSITY PRESS

London · Toronto · Melbourne

1 9 7 3

Oxford University Press, Ely House, London W.1

GLASGOW NEW YORK TORONTO MELBOURNE WELLINGTON
CAPE TOWN IBADAN NAIROBI DAR ES SALAAM LUSAKA ADDIS ABABA
DELHI BOMBAY CALCUTTA MADRAS KARACHI LAHORE DACCA
KUALA LUMPUR SINGAPORE HONG KONG TOKYO

ISBN 0 19 212962 7
© C. Walter Hodges 1973

Filmset and printed in Great Britain by
BAS Printers Limited, Wallop, Hampshire

Contents

Illustrations

The following illustrations are reproduced by the kind permission of the Trustees of the British Museum, nos. 1, 2, 3, 4, 5, 6, 7, 9, 10, 13; the Master and Fellows of Magdalene College, Cambridge, no. 8; Mr. and Mrs. Paul Mellon, nos. 12, 16, 17.

The remaining illustrations were drawn by the author.

Preface

In the summer of 1970 I was asked to advise in a project to build a full-size reconstruction of Shakespeare's Globe playhouse on or as near as possible to its historic site on Bankside. It was an imaginative scheme which for a time seemed capable of success, and the fact that it came to nothing—or at least declined into such a good imitation of coming to nothing that I am sure there cannot be any present offence in thinking so—was certainly not due to lack of enthusiasm in its authors. One day this or some similar scheme for a reconstruction may bear fruit. Meanwhile, for my part, I had been obliged for a time to consider in practical terms what steps I could seriously recommend for building a Globe which would be both useful (within its limits) and historically accurate—or, rather, in a subject peculiarly liable to conjecture, having as little recourse to conjecture as possible.

By chance, at about the same time I was also invited to read a paper dealing with the structure of Elizabethan playhouses at the First World Shakespeare Congress, held in Vancouver in 1971. For my subject I chose to attempt an orderly appreciation of the purpose and practicality of reconstructing the Globe. It may be worth recording here that at the conclusion of the Congress a resolution was passed unanimously in these terms:

Following the sessions of the First World Shakespeare Congress, the Congress wishes to encourage the hope that a studied effort will soon be made to build a full-scale reconstruction of Shakespeare's Globe Theatre. The Congress considers that such a reconstruction would be of the greatest value to Shakespearean scholarship and to the history of the Theatre, as well as of widespread interest to people and to education everywhere in the world. Because it is believed that a site very close to the original location of the Globe Theatre on Bankside in London may soon become available for development, this Congress wishes further to express its opinion that this site might be eminently suitable for such a reconstruction.

At present that Bankside site is still picturesquely crowded with its old warehouses, forming deep, wandering chasms of Victorian brick around Clink Street and the Anchor Inn. One day before very long the bulldozers will arrive, and a newly designed Bankside will be opened up and added to the landscape of modern London. It would be pleasant to imagine that a reconstruction of the Globe might in fact be allowed its place there. It would be proper. It would also be remarkable. It remains to be seen.

This book is the outcome of the preliminary studies I made for the reconstruction project, further worked upon and combined with material from my Vancouver paper. Much, obviously, remains to be done; but I have felt it would be a shame to allow the work done so far merely to be put away without being seen. It is in a condition to be judged; and who knows but one day from this point it might even be continued.

For advice and encouragement in different ways I would like to thank Professor Glynne Wickham, Professor John Russell Brown, Mr. Michael Blee, ARIBA, Mr. Anthony Tasker, ARIBA, Mr. John Rogers, and Captain Gordon J. Frost; and I am very much indebted to Mr. Tom Buckeridge for some excellent detailed photographs from the etchings of Hollar.

Convent garden S. Clement

Somerſet h. Arundel houſe Eſſex houſe Temple ſtayres Temple Black freyars

The Globe

Beere bayting h.

1

The Missing Monument

At a time near the beginning of the English Civil War, the Bohemian artist Wenceslaus Hollar, who for some years had been settled in London at the great house of his patron the Earl of Arundel, ascended to the top of the tower of the church of St. Mary Overies (now Southwark Cathedral) close by the southern abutment of London Bridge, and from that viewpoint proceeded to make a number of drawings covering the whole extent of the great city which lay before him across the river. His intention was to publish a faithfully executed panorama of this scene, from an etching he would make of it on a series of seven large plates. When printed and put together it would be offered as one of the longest, most accurate, and most comprehensive portrait views of any great city ever made. He was an expert at topographical pictures of this kind. Years before he had made a similar though smaller etching of his own native city of Prague, and it had been a print of this which had first brought him to the notice of the Earl of Arundel. One of Hollar's earliest successes after settling in England had been a similar topographical etching, on two long plates, of the view from the slopes of Greenwich Park, showing the river Thames winding its way through the middle distance towards London on the horizon. Since then he had been kept busy with every kind of illustrational and topographical work, with making etched copies of his patron's famed collection of paintings and classical sculptures, and, until recently, with his duties as drawing master to the young prince, later King Charles II. But now in these unsettled times, seeing the Trained Bands of London preparing for war, hearing rumours that the King was recruiting an army in the Midlands, and with the Earl of Arundel, his patron, away in Antwerp and by all accounts likely to remain there, Hollar must have been in some anxiety to find a new outlet for his work. Probably it was with the purpose of attracting a new public and new publishers that he had planned his spectacular

...llar: western part of the Long View of ...on, showing the Globe and Hope ...ouses. (Overall height of original print ... inches.)

Long View of London. Nevertheless for some reason the scheme was laid aside. He seems to have become busy, perhaps unexpectedly, with other work, as his many plates dating from this period attest. Besides which his domestic conditions at this time were unsettled. He had moved with his family away from the Earl's great house in the Strand, and for a while had lodgings outside London in the village of Larkhall (now swallowed up in Wandsworth). Then after a year of the Civil War we find him for a time bearing arms among the defenders of the Royalist fortress of Basing House, near Basingstoke. He was one of a remarkable garrison commanded, under the Marquis of Winchester, by a printseller turned Court portrait-painter turned soldier, one Lieutenant-Colonel Sir Robert Peake. Besides Hollar the defenders included the engraver William Faithorne, the writer Thomas Fuller (who served as chaplain), a once-fashionable comic actor William Robbins, and, surprisingly, the aged architect Inigo Jones. However, it seems that Hollar did not stay in this embattled Parnassus for very long, and he was not there, as has sometimes been asserted, when Basing House was taken and sacked by Cromwell's troops in 1645. According to his biographer Johannes Urzidil[1] he had left England in 1644 and was certainly then in Antwerp, where he had gone to find the Earl, his patron. He took with him in his portfolios all the sketches and preparatory work for the Long View of London.

It seems he cannot have travelled to Antwerp by way of Parliamentary London. Coming from a Royalist camp it is at least unlikely. Or if he did indeed go that way he cannot have taken the opportunity to notice that one conspicuous feature of his Long View had already disappeared from the scene since he was last there; or again, if he did go, maybe it was before the date of Monday April 15th, 1644. For prominently in the centre of his second plate at the western end of the View he shows us two round buildings, the Bankside amphitheatres, designated respectively 'Beere bayting h(ouse)' and 'The Globe'; whereas on the date just mentioned above, we are told that 'the Globe play house on Banks side' was 'pulled down to the ground by Sir Mathew Brand . . . to make tenements in the room of it'.[2] Clearly

[1] *Hollar: A Czech Emigré in England*, by Johannes Urzidil, London 1942, p. 41.
[2] Noted in manuscript in a copy of the 1631 edition of Stow's *Annales*, in the Folger Shakespeare Library, Washington.

Hollar was unaware of this demolition. Thus, after having settled himself in Antwerp, he eventually completed the etching of the plates of his Long View, with the Globe included. The whole work was published at last in 1647. It was not till five years later that Hollar returned to London, and doubtless by then there would have been many other changes besides the disappearance of the Globe for him to notice. It was not long before that other amphi-theatre, the Bear-baiting House, also disappeared. It had been used for the occasional baiting of the poor beasts right up to the end, but then it was 'pulled down to make tenements, by Thomas Walker a petticoat maker in Cannon Street, on Tuesday the 25th day of March 1656. Seven of Mr. Godfrey's bears, by the command of Thomas Pride, then High Sherriff of Surrey, were . . . shot to death on Saturday the 9 day of February . . . by a company of soldiers.'[1]

So, little by little, the London of the Long View was beginning to disappear even while the artist who drew it was still living in the midst of it. In another few years, and while Hollar, now an ageing man, was still there at his drawing table, all the city of his Long View disappeared in four cataclysmic days, burnt to ashes in the Great Fire of 1666. Now, therefore, having once faithfully recorded the old Shakespearian city, he took his etching needle and recorded the devastation of it. He lived long enough there-after to see the workmen clear the site of Old St. Paul's and dig the foundations for Sir Christopher Wren. He must have realized even then—and it may have been some compensation for his sadly ill-rewarded life (we are told that as he lay dying he had to beg the bailiffs not to take away the bed from under him)—that the only good and true record future historians would have of the appearance of the old cathedral would be the surviving work of his hand alone. But it would certainly have surprised him if he could have been told that history would owe him even greater thanks for his record of those two round buildings on Bankside, and especially of that one, The Globe, which he only included in his Long View because of the accident that he did not know it had just been pulled down.

It may be argued that the history of theatres is, after all, of no very great consequence in the world. From such an argument it

[1] MS. note in Stow's *Annales.*

would follow that one should not place much importance on this chance survival of a picture of the old Globe Playhouse. Even of the actors who worked there did not Shakespeare himself once say that 'the best in this kind are but shadows'? Nevertheless it can hardly be denied in the twentieth century that such shadows from stage and screen have invaded the imagination of human society to a degree even Shakespeare could scarcely have dreamed of. Reasoning from that, one may say that the theatre as an institution is the pre-eminent arrangement whereby human beings work out the models of their own conduct, their morality and aspiration, their ideas of good and evil, and in general those fantasies about themselves and their fellows which, if persisted in, tend eventually to become facts in real life. If this is so, and it would be hard to deny, then the theatre must be seen as a most powerful instrument in the social history of mankind, and its own history must therefore be allowed a corresponding importance. So it is not an exaggeration to say, as was said above, that Hollar's picture of the Globe is of even greater value to history than the many plates of his careful survey of Old St. Paul's. We naturally do not undervalue these. Nevertheless there is in England, happily, an abundant heritage of medieval churches, whereas the Globe and its few companion theatres, which were unique in their kind, have all been swept away. Hollar's chance picture is the one and only image from the hand of a reliable draughtsman which has survived.

It happens that in general the record of theatre history is well endowed with surviving examples of its historic architecture, and the public importance of these may be judged from the care with which nowadays they are restored and maintained. In some cases their survival has resulted simply from the buildings themselves being of stone, and so vast that even after several centuries of carrying away their masonry for other buildings, as happened to the amphitheatres of Classical antiquity during the Middle Ages, enough still remained on the ground for study and reconstruction. Thus we possess monumental Greek and Roman theatres, as at Epidauros and Orange and elsewhere, so numerous as hardly to need mention. Survival in other cases has been because of patronage or the protection of closed societies. The beautiful and famous theatre built by Andrea Palladio at Vicenza in 1580 for the Olympian Academy is a case in point, as is the ducal Farnese

Theatre at Parma. The latter, which was very badly damaged in the Second World War, is being restored piece for piece as it was, and the work after many years is now nearly complete. Sweden's royal palace theatre of the eighteenth century at Drottningholm is unique because with it are preserved all its original sets of painted scenery and stage working gear. Great eighteenth-century theatres and opera houses throughout Europe (as at Versailles, Salzburg, and Vienna) can be seen, after some recent refurbishing, as fine as they were when they were built. Other more modest, even very humble, examples of bygone provincial theatres have survived by the lucky chance of being as it were embalmed, by conversion to other uses, when their theatrical days were over, instead of being simply pulled down. Such is the little theatre at Richmond, Yorkshire, dating from 1788 and only recently re-claimed from its long duty as a warehouse. It preserves features of the eighteenth-century theatre which have survived nowhere else. Such also is the provincial *corral* theatre found and restored at Almagro in the Ciudad Real province of Spain. It dates from the days of Calderón and Lope de Vega. During restoration a pack of seventeenth-century playing cards was found tucked away in the recesses of one of its dressing-rooms. Even the smallest relics may turn out to have value when assembled in the right place.[1]

Thus it may be said that with only one important exception there survives in the world a series of historic theatre buildings covering every period from antiquity to the present time. They stand not only as historic monuments, but as places of living aesthetic pleasure in their own right, and wherever possible they have been restored to their original use. But the one exception is remarkable indeed. It is none other than the great theatre of Elizabethan and Jacobean London, 'the quick forge and working house' of Shakespeare himself, the theatre which was, beyond all question, the scene of the most phenomenal manifestation of the dramatic genius from the time of Sophocles until the present day, a genius which has profoundly affected the whole culture of Europe and of the civilized world. Therefore surely the physical

[1] A paragraph in *The Times* of 2 August 1972 announces the discovery by Mr. Sorensen, of the London Museum, of the original entrance doors of Astley's Circus, the famous arena which was built around 1780 and has been long demolished. The doors are being proudly reclaimed for the Museum, and are described by the finder as 'to me . . . as important as finding Tutankhamun'.

conditions of the playhouses which were devised and built for it, of which Shakespeare's own Globe must be taken as the pre-eminent example, cannot fail to be of importance in the world. Yet of this theatre, and of this only among theatres even remotely comparable in their influence, there remains neither stick nor stone to be seen. It is the most significant missing monument of theatre history. Small wonder, therefore, that every so often, and indeed with increasing frequency, proposals are made to fill the gap. The Globe should be rebuilt. What seems strange is that the rebuilding has not already been done.

One feels it certainly would have been done, if any part of the original Globe had remained to build on to, to give an absolute key for a reconstruction. Failing that, however, it has to be accepted that a reconstruction would not be simply the restoration of a ruined historic original, but a new work. Even to put it on its own former site would not now be practicable since most of that site lies buried deep under the main road approaching Southwark Bridge. But that is no matter. The structure of the original Globe itself was once moved lock, stock and barrel from Shoreditch to the Bankside site, and re-erected there, in Shakespeare's day. It makes no bad precedent for moving its successor to some other Bankside site, or even further away if necessary.

And it is hardly more difficult to justify the putting up of a new structure. Certainly in terms of sentiment it would be a loss not to be able to claim that these timbered galleries were the actual ones Shakespeare used to see, this stage the actual stage he trod. Yet the loss even of such a valued element as that does not invalidate the need for the building. It should be built for three main reasons. Firstly, *as a replacement* for the lost original, to fill the gap in the line of historic theatre buildings, as briefly described above. Secondly, as a means of aesthetic and educative research— for who would deny that a rebuilt Globe would have the greatest value for the study of problems which are still outstanding (for lack of it) in the techniques of Elizabethan staging, for education at all levels, and for the full enjoyment of this greatest English contribution to the culture of the European renaissance? And so, thirdly, it should be built as a national monument; for if there is any value at all in having monuments to great persons and great occasions, and if the worldwide renown of Shakespeare and his fellows is really so great and well deserved as we suppose, then there can hardly be an historical event more worthy of a monument than the brief remarkable flowering of the Shakespearian theatre, and hardly a monument more appropriate than to rebuild it. And there can be no doubt that if it were built it would have as great an attraction for visitors in our own time as it had in its own.

But there is one objection to rebuilding the Globe which at first sight seems indeed very powerful. It is objected that it cannot be rebuilt because we do not know well enough what the original actually looked like. It is pointed out that scholars, having worked on this problem over the past forty years, have arrived at different conclusions, many of which are strongly opposed to each other. How can any agreement be reached? Was the shape of the Globe round or polygonal? Was the stage structure arranged to provide seven distinct and permanent acting areas having specific functions, as Adams says? Did the actors all ascend to curtained stage-houses from a tiring-house underneath the stage, as Hotson avers? Or on the other hand was everything managed with a simplicity of curtained doorways such as Hosley demonstrates? Can one reconcile such opposed views? Ought one even to try? Would it not be best to leave actual reconstruction alone, and let learned speculation continue on its way unhampered by such a concrete luggage?

This objection has not anything like the force it seems to have. It is a paper tiger. For a beginning, the major dissensions are almost all concerned with the arrangements of the stage, not with the surrounding body of the house in which that stage was placed. But in that case the variety of the opposed opinions about staging provides an argument *in favour of* full-scale reconstruction rather than against it; for the stage and tiring-house arrangements could be made adjustable as a means of experimentation in those very problems which are offered as a reason for not building the experimental equipment. Few things would now be more useful in this field than to have a full-scale theatre at hand, in which to put alternative theories to the test. But more than that, the contention that we do not know what the building *looked* like is substantially untrue. We certainly have enough documentary information from different sources to allow us to proceed to a reconstruction with a great deal of confidence and no lack of scholarly discipline. Indeed in certain respects we know with a clarity approaching actual precision how it ought to be done; and though it is true that most of the exterior views of Elizabethan playhouses with which contemporary engravers have provided us are quaintly disproportioned and, without some adaptation, unacceptable, one of them is not, and that one is the one above all which we would most wish to reconstruct, the Globe itself, as it is shown to us by Wenceslaus Hollar. Only (in a way unfortunately) it is the playhouse now generally called the Second Globe, the one which began its career in 1614 following the destruction by fire of the First Globe the previous summer, which Hollar saw and drew. Unfortunately again, by an obtuseness deriving perhaps from a kind of literary sentimentality, it is the First Globe, the one with the picturesque roof of thatch which so romantically caught fire in that summer of 1613, which scholars have for so long been trying so hard to reconstruct. The First Globe was 'Shakespeare's Globe', the First Globe was the Globe of *Hamlet*, *Macbeth*, and *King Lear*, the First Globe was the darling birthplace of genius; and so naturally it is the First Globe we want so much to restore. But if we seek to reconstruct with authenticity we must work with the most authentic material available, even though it may not be quite the material we could have wished. Of the First Globe nothing remains. It was totally consumed in its fire. Map-makers' engravings of it, being only supplementary to their maps and based seemingly upon inaccurate verbal descriptions and copies of each other's mistakes, are of shaky value. Hollar's picture alone is the work of a reliable hand and eye. But (once more unfortunately) what he tells us is something we do not very much like, and find hard to accept. His Globe is an oddly-shaped, clumsy-looking building. We do not quite know what to make of it, and perhaps simply because it seems rather unattractive in itself nobody has ever tried, or at least has not tried very hard, to make anything of it in its own character at all. Yet surely, if Hollar is to be trusted, the very singularity of the building he shows suggests a riddle, and if that is so it should, like other riddles, contain the clue to its own answer. The more wonder, then, that investigation hitherto does not seem to have thought it useful to try conclusions with this sphinx. It is here to be attempted, following three preliminary questions.

First is a question deriving from what, as we have suggested above, is a rather sentimental concern that the Second Globe is not, as the First was, 'Shakespeare's Globe'. Certainly it was not the playhouse of his heyday; but can we really suppose that when the theatre which was the source of his prosperity, and in the management of which he was a senior partner, was burned down, he did not himself take a prominent part in planning the new building which was to replace it?[1] It may indeed be doubted if he had half so much influence at the planning of the First Globe as he did of the Second. And in that case the Second Globe has as much claim to be considered Shakespeare's theatre as has the First.

The second question is this: supposing the Globe had not been pulled down by Sir Matthew Brand in April 1644; supposing that some vestiges of its frame or foundations had survived the up-rootings and rebuildings of three hundred years; supposing, say, it had been incorporated into the fabric of some inn, or had become a vegetable market or a warren of slums until its last derelict parts were joyfully discovered by antiquarians in the nineteenth century, would not these remains have been preserved and properly surveyed and used as a basis for re-constructing the Globe, possibly at full scale, long before now? And if so which Globe would it have been that was thus dis-covered and rebuilt to replace the missing monument? It would of course have been the Second, Hollar's Globe. Would we not have been satisfied with that? Therefore, lacking other equally reliable evidence, should we not be satisfied with it now?

This brings in the third question. The reliability of Hollar as a witness has been consistently stressed throughout this chapter; but since it is in fact fundamental to this whole study, should it be accepted as self-evident or allowed to pass without challenge? Not everyone will think so. The quality of Hollar's testimony ought therefore to be examined more closely before we proceed further. Such will be the business of the next chapter.

---

[1] It is conventionally taught that Shakespeare 'retired' to Stratford in 1612. He may have done so, but he was back in London in the spring of 1613, buying and mortgaging property in Blackfriars, as again in 1615 on similar business. That he should not likewise have returned for the planning of the new Globe is, to put it mildly, a very improbable supposition.

2

The Credibility of Wenceslaus Hollar

In April 1636 Thomas Howard, 14th Earl of Arundel, set out from England on a mission from King Charles I to the Emperor Frederick III. He was to try to arrange the restoration of certain properties in the Palatinate once belonging to the exiled Elector Palatine, who was the King's nephew. In this respect his mission in the end turned out a failure; but the Earl was nevertheless able to make some use of the journey on his own account. He was very wealthy, a famous patron of the arts, and a great collector. Wherever he went he visited palaces and churches, printing shops and artists' studios; and he had with him in his following, besides the staff of secretaries necessary for his mission, certain writers and artists whose task it was to make a full record of his journey and the places he visited. While he was in Cologne he was much impressed by the etchings of Wenceslaus Hollar, who happened at the time to be working there, and, being himself on his way to Bohemia, he persuaded the Bohemian Hollar to go with him. A draughtsman–interpreter must have seemed to him an unusually advantageous addition to his train. The Earl was a good amateur draughtsman himself. He used to say that no man ought to be considered properly educated until he had learned to draw, and it is likely that he made some use of the opportunity to take lessons from Hollar. In any event, when his mission to Bohemia finally came to an end the Earl invited Hollar to remain with his following on their return to England; and Hollar accepted.

He arrived in England in January 1637, and lived for the next five years as a member of the Earl's household at Arundel House, on the north bank of the Thames between London and West-minster. Here he was set up in a studio with a great window facing the courtyard, and here when he was not employed in teaching or other work he had the continuing task of copying, as drawings or etchings, all the important items in the Earl's collection of paintings and antique sculpture. Also at Arundel House he met

The Credibility of Wenceslaus Hollar

Mistress Tracy, the Countess's chambermaid, who later became his wife.

From this time forward, then, except for some years of exile in Antwerp during the Commonwealth, Hollar lived as a Londoner until his death in 1677. His range of work in subject matter was prodigious and in the technique of etching remarkable. He engraved figures in costume, portraits, topographical drawings, maps, copies of paintings, animals, insects, and flowers. His elegant etchings of sea-shells were admired by Rembrandt. He was well known to a wide circle among the intellectuals of the Restoration, whose books he illustrated, and to all the publishers in London, who underpaid him. Above all, he specialized in the representation of buildings. His series of St. Paul's Cathedral has already been mentioned. He made similar surveys of Westminster Abbey and Windsor Castle. His claim in all such work was to be accurate. In his famous etching of the Royal Exchange he shows the great courtyard, full of people; but because in doing this he could show only three sides of it, and has been obliged to cut away the whole colonnade of the ambulatory at the front of his picture, he appends a note, in tiny writing along the bottom: 'The foremost is to be understood for the fourth Walke, being such as th'other three, arched and such Pillors as the rest/ All which could not bee here conveniently exprest.' The viewer is thus not misled. And of his large general view of Prague which he etched from a drawing made on the spot many years before, he takes care to reassure us in the inscription that it is 'most exactly' drawn (*Wenzeslaus Hollar . . . exactissime delineavit*). How exactly he had succeeded we cannot at this distance of time be sure; but at least we know what he intended. We seek now for something to test him by.

Let us look first at two of his little views of London depicted from the country just outside. He etched many of these small plates at different times, and the scenes when compared with each other show a remarkable consistency in their representation of particular details. The two we are now considering, however, are included simply to demonstrate a subjective convincingness in his reporting of these scenes. We may imagine ourselves to be there in that place at that time, the sketchbook as it were in our own hands. In the first (fig. 2) we are in Tothill Fields, Westminster, looking north-east. People are taking the air in the open fields

21

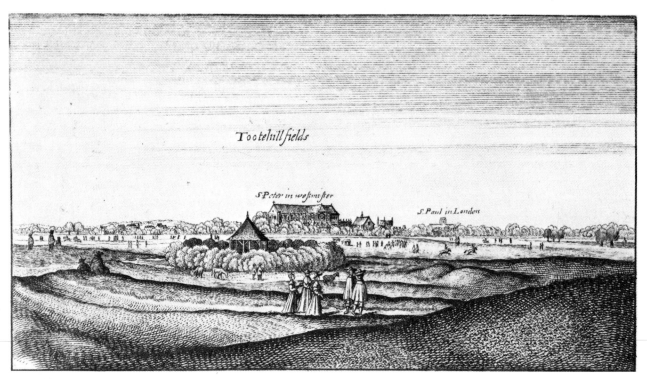

2. *Hollar: view towards London from Tothill Fields, Westminster*

where nowadays Horseferry Road and Marsham Street push their
way among the houses between Westminster Hospital and the
Tate Gallery. Horses are grazing or being galloped. People
are watching a wrestling match. In the middle distance Westminster Abbey occupies the centre of the scene. It is an unfamiliar
Abbey because it lacks its twin western towers which were not
added until the eighteenth century. To the right of the Abbey is
the steep roof of Westminster Hall, with its central lantern spire;
and to the right again, the old Parliament House which was
burned down in 1834; and then in the far distance, beyond the
curve of the river, we see above the trees the blunt tower of 'St.
Paul in London'. The point to be made is that, whatever its faults
(and it has some: for instance, Hollar seems not to have observed
the Abbey's Chapter House, which ought to have been visible
from his position unless by a trick of the light its outline was lost
against the body of the church), the picture is a direct report
upon the rural surroundings of London and Westminster, and
their visual relationship to each other at that time, which de-
mands to be believed. The same is true of the next (fig. 3), a view
entitled *On the North side of London*. This is one of several plates

22

which Hollar etched in the Plague Year of 1665. All these were drawn in the vicinity of Moorfields and Islington, and it seems likely the artist had taken lodgings there, perhaps to avoid the infection (which nevertheless tragically carried off his only son[1]). Here we see the last of Old London before it was all consumed in the Great Fire the following year. Among the parish churches which raise their towers around the bulk of St. Paul's, the crown-shaped medieval lantern tower of St. Mary-le-Bow is easily identifiable at centre left. This we are to recognize again in another picture. For the present we state, as with the previous one, that this sketch has all the character of direct reporting from a specific viewing place. A trained hand is recording directly what a trained eye is seeing, in the plainest terms.

[1] John Aubrey noted of the lad that he was 'an ingeniose youth; drew delicately'.

3. Hollar: the City, with Old St Paul's, viewed from the fields near Islington

4. The courtyard of Arundel House, looking north

We turn now to that plate of the Long View which shows the two theatres of our study, the Globe and the 'Beere bayting' (fig. 1). In the distance beyond them, on the far bank of the river, Hollar has identified Arundel House. Since this was his home for five years we must suppose that he knew what he was drawing. It will therefore be of interest to examine how far he thought it needful to achieve any sort of exactness in this distant detail.

Hollar has left us five views drawn in and around Arundel House. Two of these, which show its principal courtyard from two opposite positions, were etched during the exile in Antwerp at the time Hollar was working on the Long View of London.[1] They may have been intended as a memento for his old patron the Earl, who was himself in exile, first in Antwerp and later in Italy, where

[1] A small mystery attaches to these two etchings. They are inscribed *Adam A. Bierling delin: W. Hollar fecit 1646.* The mystery concerns this Adam Bierling who is thus credited with the drawing. According to A. M. Hind nothing is known of him except that he appears to have been Hollar's publisher for a time. (See Hind, *Wenceslaus Hollar and his Views of London and Windsor*, London 1922.) Hind thinks Bierling may have been free to visit London and obtain details at that time when Hollar was not; which is true, but rather an unlikely explanation. Perhaps he was an amateur draughtsman, and Hollar was teaching him; perhaps he worked up a preliminary drawing for the plate from Hollar's sketches; or perhaps Hollar was encouraging him for some reason with a flattering compliment. We shall not know. That the final work was Hollar's is certain enough, and most likely the first also. But the mystery remains: how and why did A. A. Bierling get into the act?

5. The courtyard of Arundel House, looking south

he died. The pictures are very evocative. In the first (fig. 4), which is a view looking north, we should note the lodging-house with the covered stairway outside. To the right of it is the top of the church tower of St. Clement Danes, in the Strand beyond; and on the right within the yard itself is the door of the painting room or picture gallery, with a great window set up in the roof. Two pictures are leaning against the wall outside the door. Still further along we must note the sundial on the wall between two upper windows and the door beneath with a pent roof. These provide a key for the next view (fig. 5), the same courtyard, but seen from the opposite direction; the door and sundial are now on the left of the picture. The sense of bustle, with coachmen, carriages and horses all preparing for a journey, and the man with hawk on wrist coming out at the door of the great hall (using a magnifying glass, it can be seen that he has come up a flight of stairs from the hall below to the upper level of the yard), all this gives a vivid impression of daily life in a nobleman's household just before the Civil War. For our purposes here we should note the roof of the great hall with the octagonal lantern set midway upon the ridge; and, to the left, between the chimneys, a glimpse of the river Thames with houses on its far side.

It is the river which next concerns us. Hollar has left us a small and remarkable panorama of *London from ye top of Arundell House* (fig. 6) which shows all the riverside scene above London

6. *Hollar: view looking east from the roof of Arundel House. On the left, the building with the steepled lantern is the hall of the neighbouring Essex House. The many-gabled building just beyond that is the Temple. (Enlarged from print 5⅜ inches wide.)*

Bridge. Identifiable buildings in this tiny frame are the Temple, with St. Paul's on the skyline beyond it, the lantern-crowned tower of Bow church, the spires of St. Laurence Poultney and St. Dunstan in the East, the Tower of London, London Bridge, and, just entering the frame on the right, St. Mary Overies in Southwark. Just below the tower of Bow church and some distance forward from it is the long roof of Blackfriars hall where Shakespeare's old playhouse of the King's Men may still have been in operation, though in its last days, when this view was taken. In the right foreground the buildings obscure the landing-stage at Milford Stairs, though we see the edge of a timber retaining-wall supporting the bank beyond it. This retaining-wall is seen again closely in our next view (fig. 7). It shows the same scene as before, but from a lower viewpoint, on the foreshore by Milford Stairs; and as if this etching were not delightful enough on its own, it has the added advantage that we can compare it point by point with the drawing from which the plate was copied (fig. 8). We see again the spires of St. Laurence and St. Dunstan, but the tower of Bow

26

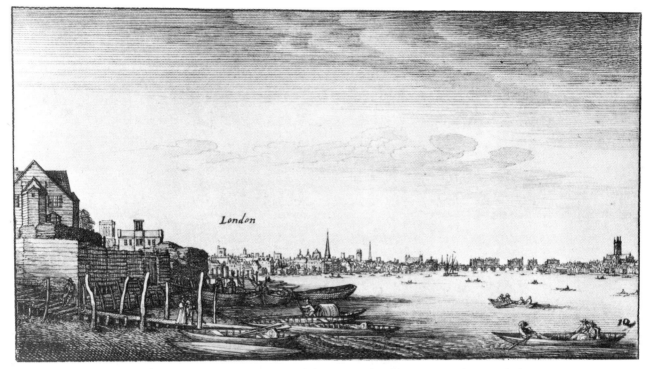

7. Hollar: *London from the foreshore by Arundel House. (Etching: 6⅝ inches wide.)*

church has disappeared, being hidden by buildings in the foreground, and the tower of St. Paul's itself is now only glimpsed low
down between two of these buildings. The fidelity of this detail of
perspective makes the picture especially convincing. On the
extreme right St. Mary Overies has now fully entered the scene.
We could wish there had been yet a little more space beyond it,

8. Hollar: *original pencil drawing for the etching at figure 7*

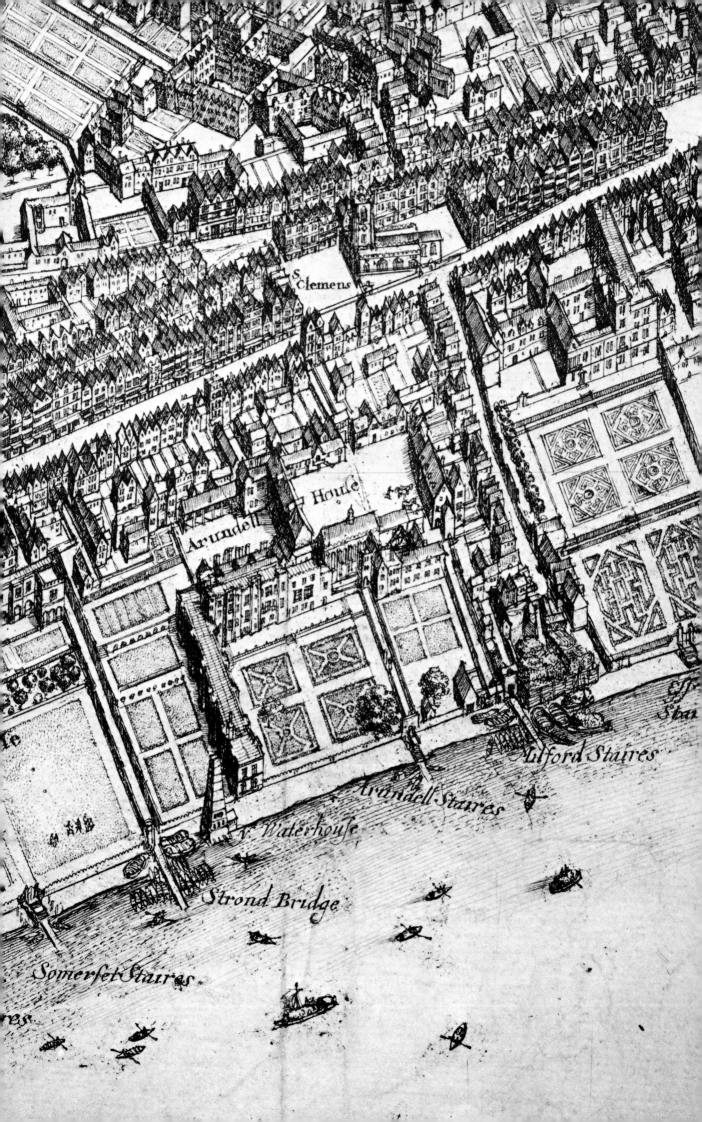

S Clemens

Arundel

House

Milford Staires

Arundell Staires

v. Waterhouse

Strond Bridge

Somerset Staires

for had there been, we might then have seen another view of the Globe playhouse, as Hollar himself must have seen it every day, across the river.

Years later he etched one more view of Arundel House. He included it in a large and detailed aerial view of all the western suburbs of London from Temple Bar to Charing Cross, and north to Holborn. The portion containing Arundel House is reproduced here (fig. 9), and we may now compare it with the other views we have been seeing, and identify their positions. We see the court-yard, with the lantern-topped roof of the great hall on the south of it. (It will be noted that the hall building appears higher on its southern elevation than on the northern side shown in fig. 5. This is because of the fall of the land towards the river, and confirms the detail already noted, that the entry to the hall from the upper level of the courtyard leads downward by a flight of steps.) On the north of the yard we see the outside staircase, and, in the Strand beyond, the church of St. Clement Danes. We can identify the position on the roof ('ye top of Arundell House') from which the first view down the river was taken; and the shore at Arundel Stairs which was the viewpoint of the second. Also to be noted is the timber retaining-wall of the bank at Milford Stairs.

This circumstantial aerial view of Arundel House may now be compared with the one in the distance in the Long View (fig. 1). Until now it has been difficult to distinguish, in all the hugger-mugger of buildings lying back from the river, which was the house itself, except for the long wing extending down to the river bank. Indeed we might be forgiven for supposing that Hollar had been content only to indicate a little and make up the rest. But now we can make it out, and for simplification the drawing here given (fig. 11) has been traced and extracted from the surrounding parts of the view. It will be noted that Hollar has drawn it with detailed care. It is clearly intended to be a reliable representation, and so it increases the credit of all the other information in the plate. Yet one thing may strike us as an important disparity. In the aerial view, at the river's edge right by Arundel House is a tall, singular, pyramidal structure identified as 'Ye Waterhouse'. It is a pumping station, and must have been the most striking landmark along the whole of that stretch of the river; and yet in the Long View it does not appear. How, then, can any part of the Long View be credited, if such a striking visual accent has been

d's eye view of Arundel House
ts surroundings c. 1660

carelessly omitted? The answer is that this 'Waterhouse' was not erected until 1655, eight years after the Long View had been published. The aerial view is a later work.

Enough has now been said to show that Hollar may be credited with at least the intention of accuracy, and it is clear that he had the technical ability to be reasonably accurate whenever he chose. It is now time to mention some of his limitations.

To begin with, he worked very rapidly. He was obliged to do so for money's sake, but he was also proud of his ability in this regard. He worked with an hour-glass before him, laying it on its side whenever he stopped, so that his clients should not be cheated; for he charged his work by the hour. (His clients seem not always to have been so scrupulous on his behalf.) However, this rapidity could mean that in some details he might rush on without a corrective second glance. Not that in his craft of commercial etching corrections would have been easy. Etching is done by the single and once-only drawing stroke of a needle upon a thin wax coating on a copper plate, which is then 'bitten' in a bath of acid. The acid bites the copper only where the pro- tecting film of wax has been scratched away. The eventual printing surface, when the wax has all been cleaned off, is thus a polished copper plate on which the image has been incised by the acid. The rolled-on printing ink is then held in this network of incised lines, and the print is taken by forcing the surface of a dampened sheet of paper into these lines with a press. It is not a process which readily offers itself for quick local emendations. It needs a very concentrated and accurate eye, and a steady skill of hand, all of which Hollar certainly had. But it would have been nothing short of miraculous if some errors did not creep in. Usually in a complicated plate these would be noted and com- pensated for where necessary by little adjustments in the neigh- bouring areas, between the key positions. Lastly it must be remembered that in drawing with his needle upon the plate the etcher is always working *in reverse*. Thus, for illustration, all the lettered titles and inscriptions that appear on Hollar's plates were actually put down on the wax back to front, looking-glass fashion. A looking-glass would, indeed, have been in continual use, and Hollar was of course well accustomed to this condition of his trade; but here and there nevertheless the translation from drawing paper to copper plate may not always have been assisted

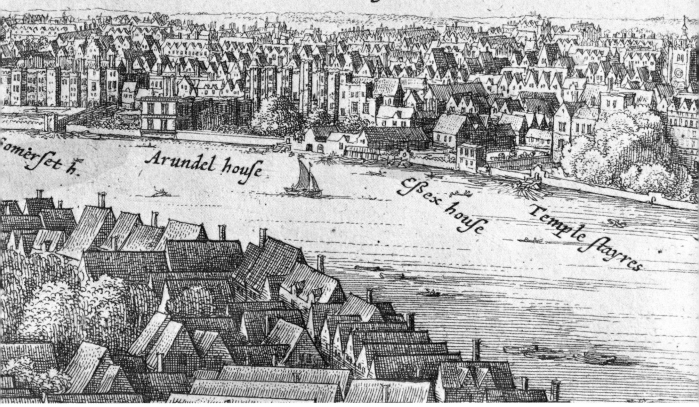

Somérset h. · Arundel house · Essex house · Temple stayres

10. *Hollar: enlarged detail of the Arundel House area from the Long View*

in the finer points of accuracy by the process of reversal.
Although the level of reliable description in Hollar's work appears
consistently high, one should be prepared to make some
allowances.

There is one building shown in the Long View of London which
was not destroyed in the Great Fire, and so can be used for
comparison with Hollar's account of it—the Tower of London.
At first sight, however, Hollar's representation of this is dis-
appointing. It is a little out of perspective with its surroundings,

Arundel house

11. *Extract traced from the Long View*

and the pictorial execution is rather perfunctory. It has, moreover, an unfamiliar look as to certain details, especially in the central keep, or White Tower. The windows shown here are all too small, and the caps to the four turrets appear different from those we see today. Apart from any defects in drawing, has not Hollar here misreported what he saw?

In fact he has not. Nearly all the original Norman windows of the White Tower were enlarged and given stone dressings around them in a partly classical style, the whole face of the building was enriched with white stone quoins, and the turret caps were replaced to an improved design under the superintendence of Sir Christopher Wren between 1663 and 1709. Hollar's report is of the building in its earlier condition. He shows a rectangular keep (which from his viewpoint is what he saw) three storeys in height, relieved with five bays of arcading on each of the sides shown. That is correct. He reports also that there were four turrets with domed caps to them in (presumably) Tudor style, that three of these were square in plan, but that the fourth, at the north-east corner, was circular. So it is. Once more he shows it correctly. In short, there is nothing substantially wrong with his account of the building either as a whole or in detail.

Thus it has been shown that, given certain reasonable allowances, Hollar's credentials as a witness are good, and that his evidence for the appearance of particular buildings shown in his Long View of London may be accepted as generally correct. We now have to examine in detail his statements about the two playhouses, the 'Beere bayting' and the Globe.

3

Hollar's Globe Examined

We have from Hollar two separate pictures showing the Globe playhouse and its neighbour the 'Beere bayting' arena, in their Bankside setting. The first is the pencil sketch (fig. 12) drawn with the actual buildings in view from the tower of St. Mary Overies. It has been partly inked over, probably but not necessarily by Hollar himself, and possibly at a later date away from the site. The second (fig. 13) is the etched version in the Long View (fig. 1) which was copied from the sketch at some unknown date prior to 1647. In the sketch the representation of the Globe is only $\frac{7}{8}$ of an inch wide; in the etching it is $\frac{3}{8}$ of an inch wide; that is, more than two and a half times the width of the sketch. Hollar may of course have used other more detailed sketches of the building, but if so none has survived. The enlarged etched version does, however, contain certain information, such as the timber framing indicated on the front wall of the gabled superstructure, which the original sketch does not show, and so must have been added from other sources, perhaps from memory.

It is here necessary to point out that it has been established beyond reasonable doubt that the names written against the two playhouses in the Long View were accidentally interchanged by Hollar at the etching stage in Antwerp, for, as can be seen, he had not indicated their names on his drawing and had evidently misremembered which was which.[1] Presumably he was not a frequenter of them. Be that as it may, the 'Beere bayting' should have been labelled as the Globe, and vice versa. We shall therefore in this study refer to them both by their proper identities, and not by the labels attached to them in the Long View print. Moreover, we shall henceforth refer to the transposed 'Beere

[1] See W. W. Braines, *The Site of the Globe Playhouse Southwark*, published for the London County Council, 1924; I. A. Shapiro, 'The Bankside Theatres: Early Engravings', *Shakespeare Survey I*, 1948; and *Bankside*: Survey of London, Vol. 22, London County Council, 1950.

bayting' (on the right) as the Hope playhouse, being the name and part-purpose given to it, as an interchangeable playhouse and baiting-ring, when it was first built.

These two buildings as seen in Hollar's etching have for so long been familiar to students of the Elizabethan theatre that the essential oddness of them both has by this time probably become overlooked. It may therefore be worth while here to draw attention to this fact. The round Globe arena with the big double-gabled superstructure of rectangular plan set in its midst, and the strange uplifted peak in the roof-ridge of the Hope, are both of them architectural curiosities with no known historical equivalents.

The problems of the Hope are certainly relevant to our inquiry and will be entered upon later; but for the present we concern

34

12. Hollar: drawing of Bankside
with the playhouses (here
reproduced at its original size)

ourselves only with the Globe. We note its principal features. The
proportionate height of the round part of the building (excluding
the superstructure) from the roof-ridge to the ground, so far as
the surrounding trees there enable us to judge it, appears to be
about one-third of the overall width. There is one continuous
range of small windows around the whole building, at a midway
height in the wall. As already noted, the double-gabled superstructure is of rectangular plan, set within a surrounding circular
one. There is a domed cupola put in what seems a rather curious
position at the rear between the gables. There are two tall,
narrow, and gabled projecting structures attached to the main
building outside, which must certainly be the housing for staircases. All those features are present in both the print and the

35

Somerset h.   Arundel house   Essex house   Temple stay

Beere bayting h.

13. Detail from
the Long View
showing the
playhouses,
enlarged

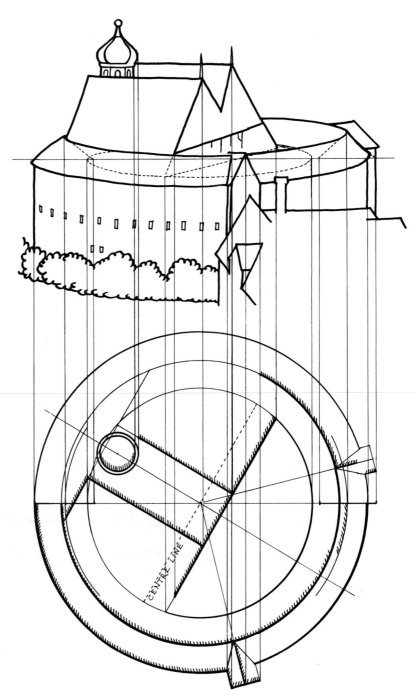

14. *Diagrammatic projection
from the etching*

preliminary drawing; but in the latter there is one additional
feature, an object rather like a tall chimney (which it cannot be)
standing up from the top of the further staircase. Most likely it
was originally intended for a flagpole, perhaps seen on a windless
day with the flag hanging down the pole and so thickening the
line; and that when this was inked over, perhaps by another hand

38

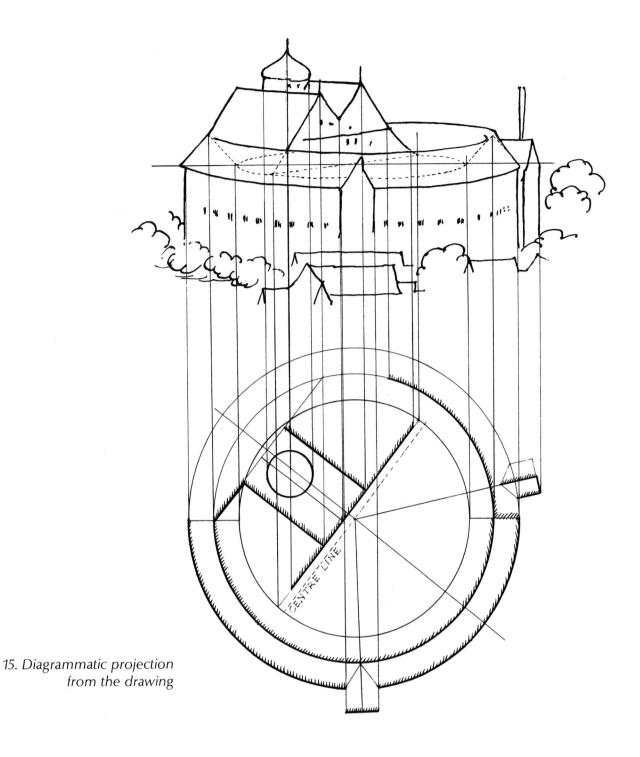

15. *Diagrammatic projection
from the drawing*

at a later date, the thing was hard to make out, and so bungled.
Whatever it is, it is an unsatisfactory item.

An important difference between the general character of the
drawing and that of the etching should be noted. The drawing has
a free and direct quality, which in the etching is lost. The latter
has a stiffer, more formal look. That is as might be expected. The

39

drawing was a spontaneous technical reaction stimulated by an immediate observation from life. The etching was a studied copy made with care in a more exacting medium, perhaps with critical adjustments from memory or other sources. Consequently there are some differences of detail and emphasis to be observed when comparing the two. These differences we are now to examine.

Two tracings have been made from photographic enlargements of the etching (fig. 14) and the drawing (fig. 15). These tracings follow the outlines of the two pictures exactly. Lines have been projected vertically downwards from the salient features of the tracings, so that their positions can be plotted on two comparative plans, here represented in circular form. (It is to be argued later that the actual plan was likely to have been polygonal rather than circular.) Certain features of the building which are out of sight in the original pictures but whose position may be reasonably estimated (e.g. the interior continuations of roof-lines, etc.) are indicated in the diagrammatic tracings by dotted lines. In the plans, all those parts of the building which are in view on the tracings are indicated by the heavier, shaded lines. All the rest is out of our sight.

We notice straight away, studying these diagrams, all manner of irregularities, inequalities, and inconsistencies. These are shown up at once by enlargement, by linear simplification, and by the removal of the camouflaging effect of light-and-shade, and are further confirmed by the translation on to the plan. We note with surprise the inequality of the two gables in the superstructure. We may take it for granted that they were not in fact unequal, but balanced, and that this therefore was an inexactitude of drawing, oddly repeated in both cases. What then of this claim for Hollar's accuracy, his reliability? Clearly we cannot push it to the verges of perfection. But the purpose of the present examination is not to discover whether or not Hollar was infallible, which it would be unreasonable to expect, but to find what fallibilities if any may have obtruded in this case, whether they are serious, and how they might be corrected. So here in the case of the twin gables, their imbalance, being enlarged and clarified and projected in plan, shows up, which in the original drawing and etching (look back upon them) went undetected. Correction here is easy.

What is of value in comparing these enlargements is to discover which of the two seems in itself to be the more convincing. It is certainly the drawing, the image rendered on the spot from the original model. As an example, compare the renderings of the roof-lines of the circular main building. In the tracing of the etching, following the pitch of the roof on each side of the circle, completing it down into the interior and projecting it on plan, we find it does not properly match. On the plan, in order to make the two sides of the roof-ridge come together in the completed circle it has been necessary to strike a median line between the two. This is not necessary in the projection from the original sketch, where the roof angles are nicely matched. Such mistakes as appear in the sketch seem more attributable to the after-work with the pen, a rather blunt instrument for so small a scale, than to any other cause—and one must certainly chalk up a bad mark for carelessness on the farther staircase-gable, where the face of the gable is shown turned towards us, which, as the plan shows, could not have been the case.

The most important matter to be decided from these pro-jections is the true position within the building of the front wall of the superstructure. We have already noted the irregularity of the twin gables, and we can tell from their positions in relation to the fore-and-aft centre line on the plans what adjustments need making. But for the frontal wall of the superstructure another, different, judgement is required. The plan-projection from the etching shows this wall standing forward from the transverse centre line. On the projection from the sketch it is a little distance behind it. Which of the two should we follow?

Our former judgement—that of the two, in a general way, the sketch is likely to be more reliable than the etching—is here reinforced by common sense. Whatever the purpose of this great superstructure roof may have been—which we shall inquire into shortly—it is reasonable to suppose it should not have obstructed more daylight than necessary from the principal source of light in this daylight theatre, the great opening overhead. The super-structure as shown in the etching would close up more than half that space; that in the sketch rather less than half. Now the stage, in theatres of this type, if we are to judge from the stipulation made in Henslowe's contract for building the Fortune, as well as from other circumstances concerning the stage area, extended from the rear wall of the stage on the actors' side of the theatre 'to the middle of the yard of the said house' (says the Fortune contract) and the overhead roof was required to cover it.[1] The Hope contract stipulates that 'the Heavens' (as the covering was called) was to be built 'all over the said stage'. Thus if Hollar's Globe followed custom in this respect we should suppose that the forward line of the Heavens superstructure ought to be set just across the *middle* of the round yard, and not either forward or rearward of it. Structural considerations, too, lend force to this conclusion, as we shall see later. We must suppose therefore that Hollar found some difficulty in getting this detail precisely right, and that in his sketch he has drawn the superstructure a little too far back. One can imagine he may even have noticed this as he was drawing it, for his line on the right side of the double-gabled roof bends itself outwards a little as it goes down, as if trying to reach a point further out along the eaves of the yard, which it ought to but doesn't quite meet. In the etching, on the other hand, he has over-amended by taking the whole too far forward.

Must we then follow our former demonstrations of Hollar's general reliability by seeking to excuse him for these and other particular inaccuracies? It would be owlish indeed to do so— unfair even to the quality of owlishness, for what owl in his right mind would take a sledgehammer to crack a nut? No two free-hand drawings of the same subject by the same hand, however skilful, will or ever can be quite the same—which is to say that some inexactitudes must be present in all. With most artists these little irregularities tend to fall into personal patterns of their own, dictated perhaps by tricks of eyesight or habits of the hand. The purpose of our diagrammatizing here is chiefly to discover what inconsistencies may have occurred between Hollar's two renderings of the Globe, and to reconcile or correct them. They are not many, and such as they are, are nearly all connected with

[1] The extant contracts for building the Fortune and the Hope playhouses, which reside with the Henslowe Papers in the archives of Dulwich College, are the essential controlling reference for structural and dimensional details of the Elizabethan and Jacobean public theatres (though in some important respects of detail they are unfortunately incomplete). The contracts are reprinted in full in most standard works on the Elizabethan stage, and in this author's *The Globe Restored* (2nd edn., Oxford University Press, 1968). For the special purpose of the present work, however, it is hoped to avoid the necessity of repeating such general information about the Elizabethan theatre as may readily be obtained elsewhere, though references will be given where needed, and it will not be assumed that the reader is already apprised of necessary background information.

drawing the perspective of the great twin-gabled roof in relation to the circle which cradles it, a problem full of little traps and deceptions, as this writer, who has now himself spent some time setting it out with square and compasses and other artificial aids which Hollar almost certainly was not using, begs leave to report. Adjustments to Hollar's irregularities may all be made either by obvious corrections of alignment or by taking middle courses between small deviations. In any case, with or without adjustments, the overall statement Hollar makes about the building is clear and unequivocal. Assuming as we now do that his statement is to be trusted as a whole and as it stands, the question next to be decided is what it may mean.

Before leaving this part of the analysis we should note in passing the position of the cupola between the gables. In both versions when projected on to the plan, this is shown to stand just forward and clear of the encircling frame of the building, overhanging the yard. We shall refer to this later.

4

Proportion, Shape and Size

In both of Hollar's pictures the Globe and its companion the Hope are shown as circular buildings. Some but not all other versions of these, in maps and panoramas of the time, show them as polygonal. Next to Hollar, the best-known contemporary print of them is that by Visscher, in the foreground of his panorama of 1616, which shows them as octagonal. On the other hand, Johannes de Witt's description of the Swan playhouse, which accompanies his famous sketch of the interior, says that it was 'built of a concrete of flint stones'. That of course refers to the outer wall only (the galleries within being of wood), and if the Second Globe had been similarly constructed it would presumably have been circular also. But the First Globe was certainly not 'round', for it was built all of wood, and so was entirely destroyed when it burned down, leaving, as witnesses tell us, nothing above ground but the piles it was built upon. Wood may indeed be fashioned into round smooth curves or any other shape you please for smaller and particular purposes; but it is surely out of the question that the timbers would have been so expensively and so unnecessarily shaped for a whole building, especially one so large as the Globe. It was most likely to have been polygonal therefore, as also was the Hope, by the same argument and from the builder's contract, which directly specifies a timber construction. Yet Hollar's picture of the Hope (which is, remember, the 'Globe' of the Long View) shows this, too, as circular. Moreover he shows the encompassing *roofs* of both the Hope and the Globe as if they were circular, which, no matter what shape the rest of the building, they would certainly not have been. Roofs are not made so. Beyond doubt, whatever the shape of the buildings under them, the roofs must have been made of straight lengths of timber formed together into a polygon, as was the whole frame of the Hope and, most likely therefore, of the Globe also. In any case the timber galleries within would have been polygonal, and it would have been

44

reasonable and in keeping with the nature of the whole building to maintain its polygonal character in the outer wall. What Hollar did in his drawing was for simplicity's sake to set down the overall appearance of what he saw, omitting in his tiny less-than-an-inch sketch the needless confusion of the slight shallow angles of the polygon. What he saw, we must suppose, was a polygon of so many sides as to be *in effect* circular. For such an effect, how many sides would be required?

We here suggest that the number of sides was sixteen—a hexadecagon. The argument for this is first, that such a figure would produce the effect in question, and second, that it is the most straightforward figure a Jacobean master-carpenter, working by traditional methods and rules-of-thumb, would be likely to have arrived at. To produce a simple octagon was a normally taught practice of the craft. The next step beyond that would simply be to halve the angles of the octagon, thus producing the sixteen-sided figure. Of course a figure of twelve sides would also have been possible, derived from an original hexagon. But whether or not it is more complicated to set out a hexagon than an octagon, it is certainly a less common (and so less traditional) building plan. Moreover a twelve-sided figure would have given a slightly less circular general effect, having more emphatic corners, which Hollar might then have thought it necessary to show. On the whole, the *most likely* plan is the sixteen-sided one. In this inquiry we shall make it a principle wherever we are presented with a choice of alternatives to adopt whichever is the most simple and direct. It is true that by this method we shall fail to catch those effects which may have been produced by cranky, devious, or exceptional minds, but since there are by definition fewer of these than of the ordinary, we are, by opting for the ordinary, more likely to stay between the borders of the right path. In the present case, since the most simple and direct figure to arrive at is in our opinion the sixteen-sided one, we shall adopt and proceed upon it without more ado.

Having thus decided upon its shape, we come next to the size of the building, and here at once we find ourselves confronted with a flat statement quite at variance with what is normally taught. Our knowledge of the dimensions of Elizabethan theatres is derived from and controlled by those of the Fortune, a square playhouse built in 1600, and to a lesser degree (because the basic

16. Hollar: the Globe, detail from the drawing (enlarged approximately × 3)

information is less complete) from the polygonal Hope of 1613. These dimensions are taken as standard simply because by chance we know them from their (extant) contracts. But what is clear from the Hollar pictures is that the Globe was bigger than either of these. With the Hope we can ascertain this by using a pair of dividers, whereby both the etching and the drawing will demonstrate that the Globe was wider than the Hope by a third (drawing) or a quarter (etching). True, we have to take into account the effect of perspective, for the Hope was further away from Hollar's original drawing position than the Globe. But it was so only by a little, not enough at that distance to account for so large a discrepancy. But Hollar may have erred? True again, to some degree he may have; but this is a wider margin of error than would seem reasonable to suppose in this case.

We must here pause briefly to note the Fortune and Hope dimensions. The Fortune externally was 80 feet square. It had

46

17. Hollar: the Hope, detail from drawing (enlarged approximately × 3)

three superimposed galleries around its yard, these being respectively 12, 11, and 9 feet in height, plus a brick foundation of 1
foot above ground, plus (presumably) an addition of, say, $1\frac{1}{2}$ feet
to account for the thickness of the floor-joists between the two
upper galleries, thus giving a total height, from ground to eaves,
of 34 feet 6 inches (or 33 feet if the joists may be supposed to
have been included in the overall gallery heights specified). The
bottom gallery was $12\frac{1}{2}$ feet wide. The two upper galleries each
had an overhang of 10 inches forward into the yard from the one
below it. Thus the width across the yard at ground level was
55 feet, and at the top gallery 51 feet 8 inches.

The dimensions given for the Hope are fewer. The lowermost
gallery was the same height as the Fortune's. The heights of the
upper two galleries are not given, but it is reasonable to suppose
that, as at the Fortune, they decreased by approximately the same
amount.

47

Now although the width or diameter of the yards of these open-yarded public theatres might vary by any amount at all, the gallery heights would not vary by much. They would not normally be any higher than they needed to be for a calculable headroom, and they must be high enough for a calculable number of rows of spectators stepped up behind each other to be able to see, reasonably well, most of the stage area and such upper parts of the façade at the back of the stage as were normally used in the action of plays. In brief, the vertical dimensions of most public playhouses with three galleries (and thus of the Globe) could not have been very different from those of the Fortune. If a theatre were more open, that is wider across the yard, the sight-lines from the galleries would become more horizontal and so the galleries could each be slightly less high.

If this is so, and if we are to accept the general validity of Hollar's evidence, then it may be demonstrated by a simple diagram that the Globe must indeed have been a larger building than the Fortune. Fig. 18 shows the elevational proportions of the Fortune from the dimensions given in the contract. It also shows the proportions of the main building (excluding superstructure) of the Globe, drawn to the same scale and calculated so as to approximate visually to Hollar's pictures of it. The chief difficulty in making this estimation is that nowhere in Hollar can one see the actual point where the walls meet the ground, because of the shrubs and trees which surround his building at the foot; but one

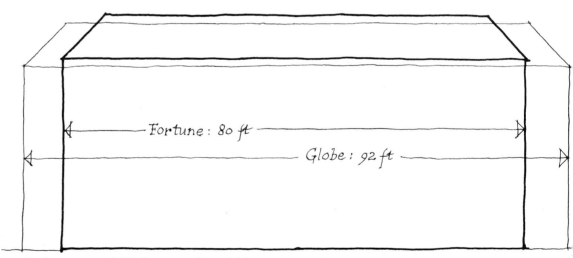

18. Fortune and Globe: exterior widths compared

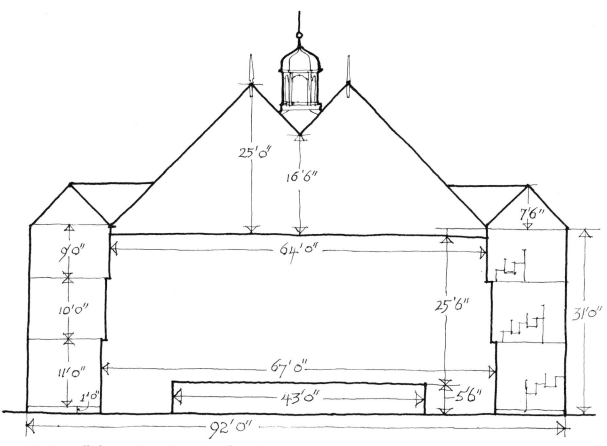

19. *Overall dimensions, interior elevation*

can calculate it fairly well. One may also take a little help, for
checking purposes, from the heights of the neighbouring houses,
which we may suppose to average about 25 feet to their roof
ridges—a safe general calculation for a two-storey timber house
of the period. One sees how high the Globe stands above them.
With all these things in mind we have calculated the principal
overall dimensions of Hollar's Globe as follows: height from
ground to eaves, 31 feet; overall diameter, 92 feet; diameter of
yard, at ground 67 feet 4 inches, and at top gallery level (the
space being decreased by the gallery overhangs) 64 feet. Although
we have made the height of the galleries slightly less than the
Fortune, the width of the yard at its widest is considerably
greater, and had we not reduced the height it would have had to
be greater still. This calculation, though it may seem surprising, is
borne out by another detail observable in Hollar and consistent
with reasonable expectation. The two staircase-towers shown on
the outside of the Globe, which at first sight seem unusually
narrow, would, on the basis of the estimated dimensions given

49

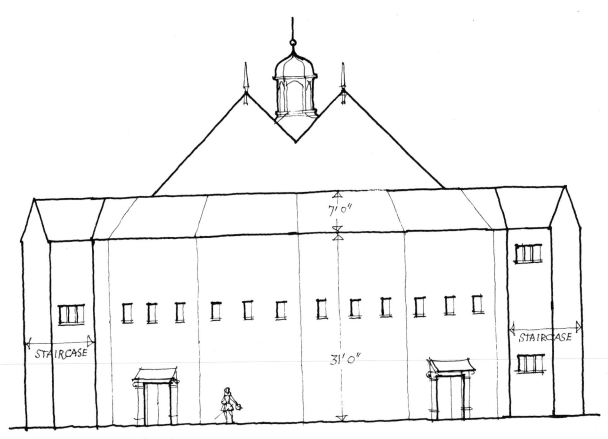

20. *Exterior: front elevation*

above, have been about 9 feet wide. This could well have housed a dog-leg staircase with half landings, each flight being approximately 3 feet 6 inches wide. Such a staircase would be correct for the constructional practice of the time. The proportion of the staircase housing shown by Hollar in fact helps to confirm, at the same time, both the reliability of Hollar's evidence and the large scale and span of the building as here postulated.

Though it cannot of course be contended that the overall dimensions given above are inch for inch actually those of the Second Globe, they do give us a *visually* right proportion, and with it a proper and valid scale within which to work. Moreover, with such a scale one may now more easily accept as factual, and not as sensational exaggeration, that contemporary account which tells of the very large audiences which the Second Globe was able to hold. The Spanish Ambassador Coloma, writing to King Philip IV's minister Olivares about the performances of Middleton's anti-Spanish-Match play *A Game at Chess* given at the Globe in 1624, reported that 'the King's men . . . are still acting

50

in London a play which so many people come to see that more than three thousand were there on the day the audience was smallest'. And later in the same report: '. . . during these last four days more than twelve thousand persons have all heard the play of *A Game at Chess* (for so they call it). . . .' In this connection it should also be remembered that Johannes de Witt in his account of the Swan in 1596 declared that that was 'the largest and most distinguished' of the London playhouses at that date, and that it had 'space for three thousand persons'. Maintaining, as scholars have had to do, a conscientious adherence to the hard evidence of the Fortune/Hope dimensions, it has been difficult to see how such numbers could possibly have been accommodated. Seeing, however, as we now do, that the Second Globe and (presumably) the Swan were larger buildings than either the Fortune or the Hope, the matter becomes more credible. Moreover, it has even to be considered that the First Globe of 1599–1613 may have been built to the same scale, for there is a witness of 1634 who describes the Second Globe as having been 'built with timber about 20 years past upon an old foundation'. Professor Bentley, having pointed out the fact that these foundations, being on marshy ground, consisted of piles which remained after the fire, observes, surely correctly, that they would have been used, as the 1634 witness states they were, for the new building.[1]

[1] G. E. Bentley, *The Jacobean and Caroline Stage*, vol. 6, p. 183.

5

The Superstructure: A Problem

Given the span that has here been estimated, we come now to consider what is in every sense the central problem of this reconstruction, the great twin-gabled superstructure standing over the middle of the yard. It was itself as big as a moderate-sized house, as may be seen by comparison with all around. How then was it supported and held in position?

Ever since research into the structure of Elizabethan theatres began towards the end of the eighteenth century it has been known that there was something variously called a 'cover' or a 'shadow' or a 'Heavens' above the stage. The old engraved views of the playhouses, their exteriors only, showed hut-like buildings poking up out of the middles of their round, open yards, but it was hard to know what these were for. Hollar's double-roof was known, but was nowhere understood or accepted on its own terms. Then in 1888 the copy of Johannes de Witt's famous sketch of the Swan interior was discovered in the university library at Utrecht, and with this, consistent as it is at all points with the exterior views, the matter of the Heavens was at last considered to be more or less cleared up. Two great posts of classic form with moulded bases, swelled shafts, and carved capitals stood upon the stage, upholding the stage roof and the overhead hut wherein was housed the winding-gear for theatrical flying effects. Charming and peculiar, this pair of pillars quickly became, perhaps more than any other feature, the outstanding and typifying visual characteristic of an Elizabethan public playhouse as it was henceforth to be generally represented. De Witt's two posts became almost the stars of the show. I myself—for it may be less ambiguous from now on if 'the writer' abandons the cover of that discreet formula and comes into the open—I myself have enjoyed making the most of them in drawings and paintings I know not how many times, and I cannot doubt that they existed. I have sometimes doubted, though, whether they were as little of a

52

nuisance on the stage as many writers on Elizabethan methods of play production have supposed, who have offered the idea that they were commonly made use of as trees and maypoles and the like. So they may have been, but I feel that they were nevertheless an obstruction in the way of sight and action which the actors would have preferred to have been rid of, had it been possible. When they worked indoors at the 'private' theatres, as Shakespeare's company did at the Blackfriars from 1608 onwards, they were not encumbered with them, and surely they must have been glad of it.

However, there on the public stages the pillars were, and very fine to look at, upholding the hut and rooflet over the stage. Then in 1613 the Globe burned down, hut, rooflet, pillars and all, until in the following year it stood rebuilt in the form we know from Hollar, a building explicitly described by several witnesses as being a great improvement upon its predecessor. 'It was', says Edmond Howes, 'new builded in far fairer manner than before.'[1] Also, 'I hear much speech of this new play-house', writes John Chamberlain to Lady Alice Carleton, on 30 June 1614, exactly one year after the fire, 'which is said to be the fairest that ever was in England.' It was new, it was better, and it had this great building overhanging the yard. But is it possible to believe that such an overbuilding was still supported, as the former hut and rooflet had been, only by two posts standing upon the stage? How many such posts must have been needed to carry such a weight, if it had all to be supported from below? And if more than two posts had been required, how could a stage thus encumbered have been thought to be as good as, let alone better than, its predecessor (for one must suppose that a general report about the theatre being 'the fairest that ever was' would include the meaning that its stage arrangements were at least no worse)?

I think it is neither reasonable to suppose nor in any way likely that there would have been more than two Heaven-supporting posts upon the stage; and with such a superstructure it is at first sight hard to imagine how only two could do the job unaided, or, if they did, how to avoid their being so massive that they would overpower the stage and the view of the play. Indeed it becomes difficult to imagine whereabouts they should stand to do their job

[1] Howes's continuation to John Stow's *Annales . . . of England,* 1615.

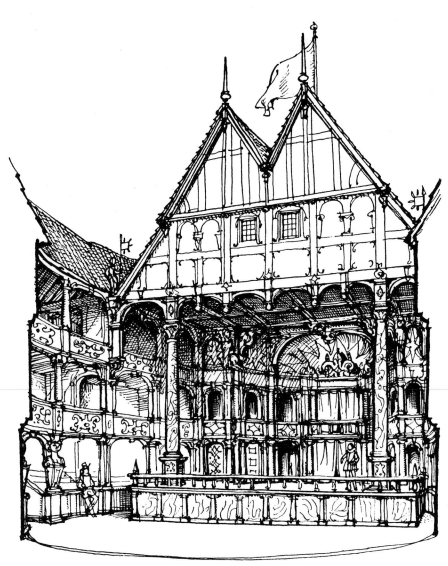

21. The Heavens supported by pillars: an earlier reconstruction

effectively. In a previous work I briefly attempted to tackle the problem, and published the drawing which, for convenient reference, I reproduce here (fig. 21). But even so I was not entirely satisfied with that result. I had a feeling that I had drawn the pillars too slender for their height and purpose, and that having brought them to the forward edge of the superstructure, to make them support the floor-joists overhead, I had had at the same time to move them as far as I could to the sides, to avoid standing them too much in the way of the audience; and thus their effectiveness was still further reduced. All in all, I felt, looking at the picture later, that these two pillars were not doing as much to support the superstructure as the superstructure was doing for

54

itself by its attachment to the sides of the main building. What, then, might happen, I asked myself, if those posts were not there at all? How much would fall if they were removed?

And at this point another question presents itself: what after all was the purpose of that same solid-looking twin-gabled building over the stage? The theatrical flying apparatus which had formerly been housed in the much smaller overhead hut shown in de Witt's sketch had surely not increased so vastly that it needed so much more room? And merely to cover over more of the yard for shelter from the weather would not have needed a structure of such a bulk as this. For what, then, was the thing designed? Is it not at least possible that it was designed not to be supported, *but to be self-supporting*?

Seen from the outside, in Hollar's view, the superstructure has all the appearance of a house; so much so, indeed, that one may easily and naturally imagine it to have floors and rooms in it. I have been describing it here as a 'structure' and a 'building', words which carry with them more the idea of a house on solid ground than, say, of a bridge or an open roof. But our exercise has already gone some way towards demonstrating the fallacy of the house idea. To the question asked above—if the two posts were removed, how much would fall?—the answer must surely be, first of all the floor (i.e. the ceiling over the stage in my early drawing). What then would be left, if that fell away, would be an open hollow shell, a roof, its rafters and trusses leaning together supported from the sides. What I am here proposing, therefore, is that the superstructure was not the house it appears to be but simply a great open timber roof, the front of which was covered across with a screen-wall to keep out wind and weather. Inside it was all hollow, and anyone standing on the stage below could have looked up and seen directly into the huge framework of the vaulting.

But could such a thing have been done? Could or would a London carpenter at that time have erected such a roof across such a span, a diameter, by our reckoning here, of no less than 64 feet? Daunting though it might seem, it could certainly be done where necessary. The great roof of Westminster Hall, built by Hugh Herland two hundred years before the Globe, has a span of 68 feet. It is a remarkable and exceptional example, certainly, but there it stood in Shakespeare's day as it stands today. In theatre building, at the Schouwburg in Amsterdam, built by Jacob van Campen in 1658, the whole roof was carried on two great horizontal beams 62 feet long, unsupported over 51 feet.[1] Again perhaps an exceptional example, constructed later than the Globe, and not in England: but it could be and was done. Moreover, looking at the double-roof system at the Globe one begins to have the impression that the two sides are locked together at the centre of the span upon a scissors principle, as if designed to prevent falling. I will try to show, below, how this might operate. Meanwhile, in case it may here be protested that I am still talking in terms of some exceptional or unusual arrangement instead of a commonplace or everyday carpentering job such as we might suppose would have been more readily available to the Globe management—that is to say, in case of an objection that such a proposition would make of the Globe a quite unique building—I can only answer that, according to the evidence, so it was. We see it in Hollar as a most unusual edifice. If it was not unique, where have we seen its like?

However, leaving that matter to stand for a while, it may here be useful and appropriate to recall something of theatre history.

In 1608, as we have said, the shareholding syndicate of the King's Men,[2] the company at the Globe, took over the management of a second playhouse at Blackfriars, on the other side of the river, within the City boundary, and near to the fashionable western suburb with its noblemen's houses along the Strand. The players had prospered at the Globe. They had achieved royal patronage. They had earned and enjoyed a regular following of gallant, sophisticated, and patrician society, and this patronage was increasingly represented in the character of their repertoire. Now the opportunity had presented itself to cross the river and play for their wealthier patrons in the greater comfort of an indoor playhouse. This venture prospered as the other had done. The Globe continued to attract the great city public; but the Blackfriars, although even when it was crowded to the doors its capacity was much smaller, was now the playhouse which set and reflected the style and taste of the time. New plays were given first at the Blackfriars and were then transferred to Bankside,

[1] See *The Globe Restored* (1968), plates 52–54.
[2] Richard and Cuthbert Burbage, William Shakespeare, John Heminges, Henry Condell, William Sly, and Thomas Evans.

carrying with them the acclaim of the nobility and gentry, to satisfy the multitudes at the Globe. For this reason, as Professor Wickham has pointed out, there cannot have been any radical difference between the staging arrangements at the two play-houses.[1] The principal physical difference was simply that at the Blackfriars there was a roof, which provided not only shelter but the possibility—indeed, often the necessity—of artificial lighting. The covered 'private' Blackfriars was now the company's winter theatre, and the open 'public' Globe its summer one.

The Blackfriars had first been fitted up as a theatre for the use of a company of boy players thirty-two years before the King's Men took it over. It was located in the Upper Frater or refectory of the old Dominican friary, a great hall 100 feet long and 46 feet wide, which (as reconstructors generally agree) must have been covered by its original medieval open timber roof.[2] In Hollar's Long View (fig. 1) we can see, beyond 'The Globe' (i.e. the Hope) on the far side of the river, just back from the shore to the right of Black-friars, a long, steep roof which can hardly be other than that of the old friary. We have seen it before, from another direction, in Hollar's view 'from ye top of Arundell House' (fig. 6). Under that roof was the playhouse.

As we have seen, when the first Globe was destroyed in the afternoon of June the 29th, 1613, the company lost no time in rebuilding it. The new Globe was planned, financed, built, and opened for business within a year. Moreover, it was 'builded in far fairer manner than before'. The 'Water Poet' John Taylor wrote:

> As Gold is better that's in fire tried,
> So is the bankeside Globe that late was burn'd:
> For where before it had a thatched hide,
> Now to a stately Theator is turn'd.
> Which is an Emblem, that great things are won,
> By those that dare through greatest dangers run.

[1] Glynne Wickham, *Early English Stages*, vol. 2, part II, 1972, p. 137.
[2] For details of the Blackfriars Playhouse the reader should consult: Irwin Smith, *Shakespeare's Blackfriars Playhouse*, London 1966; Glynne Wickham, *Early English Stages*, vol. 2, part II, London 1972; Richard Hosley, 'A Reconstruction of the Second Blackfriars', printed in *The Elizabethan Theatre*, ed. David Galloway, Toronto 1969; and G. E. Bentley, *The Jacobean and Caroline Stage*, vol. 6, Oxford 1968.

Thus having been obliged to lay out their money on a new building, the company took this obvious opportunity to make certain improvements, guided, as we may suppose, by thirty-seven years' experience as the actors and managers of the world's first commercial public theatres. What, then, were these improvements? Some must have been aimed at increasing the comfort and convenience of the auditorium, some to give the interior a more 'stately' and 'far fairer' appearance than before. One we know concerned the roofing: the 'thatched hide' which had caused the fire at the first Globe was here replaced with tiles. At the same time it would seem that the whole roof over the stage was increased from the elementary hut-and-rooflet of the earlier theatres to the large structure shown in Hollar. This, I suggest, was an improvement prompted by the company's experience at the roofed-in Blackfriars. They would now try to provide at their large public theatre as much cover as possible. They could not cover all the open yard because, apart from any other structural problems this would have involved, it would have excluded too much light; but they could cover a full half of it. That would be a definite improvement. It would be an even greater improvement, if only it could be done, to get rid of those two great posts standing upon the stage. There was no such obstruction on the stage at the Blackfriars. The Burbages could have taken their builder there and, pointing up to the trusses of the medieval roof overhead, said to him: Can you not contrive to give us something like that?

What is certain is that whether or not they or their builder at that time thought the posts could be done away with, another management nearby was convinced that they could. Hardly had the smoke cleared from the wreckage of the old Globe before Philip Henslowe, proprietor of a competitive establishment two hundred yards down the lane, had seen his opportunity and with his partner Jacob Meade set about to take advantage of it.

At an earlier period, before the accession of James I, Henslowe's company had been a good match for the Burbage company (the Chamberlain's Men) in the leadership of the London theatre. Henslowe had the advantage that his son-in-law and partner, Edward Alleyn, was then the most renowned actor of the day. But in 1599 the Chamberlain's Men erected their first Globe on Bankside close to Henslowe's smaller, older, and presumably less attractive theatre, the Rose. Then in 1604 Alleyn retired from the stage, and soon after that the Rose seems to have gone out of business. The Chamberlain's Men, with Shakespeare and Richard Burbage, were now reaping all the theatrical harvest of Bankside more or less uncontested. Henslowe had his other theatre, the Fortune, in the Clerkenwell district; but on Bankside his interests were now confined to bull- and bear-baiting. But his arena for this, and also the sheds and kennels where he kept his beasts, seem all to have been in need of renovation by the time the neighbouring Globe suddenly went up in flames. It was therefore only common prudence for Henslowe and Meade to decide that now, while their competitors were out of business and rebuilding their premises, was the time to set their own house in order. On the 29th of August, exactly two months after the Globe fire, they signed a contract with the carpenter Gilbert Katherens, who was to pull down their old bear-baiting arena with all its stables and kennels, and re-erect them new. This was to be the Hope play-house for which we have extant both the contract and Hollar's picture. But the arena at the Hope was to be made not solely for animal-baiting, but for an alternative use as a playhouse—a 'Game place or Playhouse fit and convenient in all things, both for players to play in, and for the game of Beares and Bulls to be bayted in the same'. It was to have a 'Tire house and a stage to be carried or taken away' so that the arena could be left clear when-ever needed for the 'game of Beares and Bulls'. This stage was 'to stand upon trestles good substantial and sufficient for the carrying and bearing of such a stage'. And then it was enjoined that Katherens 'shall also build the Heavens all over the said stage, to be borne or carried *without any posts or supporters to be fixed or set upon the said stage*'. (My italics.)

It is possible to argue that although the posts were not to be set upon the stage, which would have interfered with the stated purpose of carrying the stage away, they might nevertheless have stood somewhere else in the arena. It is even possible with a generous stretch of credibility to accept an argument that such posts would not have interfered too seriously with the game of bear-baiting; but for the free movement of bull-baiting it is quite impossible to think so. It has to be accepted absolutely that no supporting posts could have been put anywhere in that arena, and that Henslowe's Heavens at the Hope were carried 'all over' the stage area without any such support at all.

The fact that concerns us at this moment is not so much how it could have been done but that it was done at all, and that Henslowe had been convinced it could be done. From the evidence we have, he was not the sort of man to lay out his money on untried experiments, but rather the opposite. He liked to copy what others had already tried successfully. In his contract for the Fortune (1599) he specified that the stage there must be copied from the one at the recently erected First Globe. In his contract for the Hope he specified that its 'compass, form, wideness and height' was to be copied from the Swan. Where, then, did he get the idea that his Heavens at the Hope could and should be supported or carried without any posts set upon the stage?

Was it his own idea? If so, why should not the Globe management have taken a leaf out of his own book, and copied him? Or might it not have been, on the other hand, that having learned of something new that was being planned for the new Globe, Henslowe was deciding to keep up with the times and copy the innovation? To me this latter seems more likely, though it is a subjective notion and therefore may not take us far. Also, against it, at first sight, is the observation that in Hollar the Globe and the Hope appear with two very dissimilar superstructures: the former with its great twin-gable, the latter with only its quaint and curious peak. But as I shall show later, this ultimately turns out to be a distinction without a difference. Therefore, for present purposes, I shall continue with the hypothesis that however dissimilar the two may appear, the Globe's superstructure had one thing at least in common with the Hope's—that each was carried over the stage without being supported by posts.

6

The Superstructure: A Solution

The design and construction of large open timber roofs was one of the crowning achievements of medieval carpentry, and in this skill the English carpenters were pre-eminent. The roof of Westminster Hall was completed in 1399, and is still today one of the largest timber roofs in the world unsupported by pillars. A plentiful supply of English oak and a skilful imagination in the use of it for hammer-beams, camber-beams, scissor-beams, king- and queen-posts, collars and braces, provided for the roofs of great halls and churches throughout the country a variety of structural invention without equal in its kind. This tradition of building did not die out after the achievement of its greatest examples: it remained always on hand. The carpenters who had completed the double-hammer-beam roof at Middle Temple Hall in 1572 were many of them still alive when their next generation was erecting the double-gable over the Globe.

The science of timber roofing in England was such that no metal was used anywhere in the construction. Roofs were held together solely by the use of wooden pegs, subtle joinery, and true balance. If a roof were not properly balanced it would lay an unequal strain upon its pegs which in time would be shorn through. The roof would then sag; but it would not fall. Fred H. Crossley quotes an instance of a 500-year-old roof which had rotted because of bad ventilation and damp, and which 'was found to be holding itself together without tenons which had completely decayed, and was apparently suspended in position under its own volition until it was interfered with'.[1] The sag of a pitched roof if properly designed would in effect cause its two halves to lean more heavily together, thus still supporting itself by its own compression. The pressure thus created would transfer itself downwards on to the supporting walls, attempting to thrust

[1] *Timber Building in England from Early Times to the End of the Seventeenth Century*, 1951, pp. 56–7.

61

them outwards. A pitched roof is thus supported by the balance of its pressures and by resistance to its thrust. The traditional methods of countering thrust were either to buttress the walls, or to give a steep pitch to the roof (thus carrying most of the weight more directly downwards than outwards); or both.

At the Globe the problem of thrust was overcome not by the pitch of the roof but by the unusual width of the walls which supported it—for, in relation to the great roof, the surrounding galleries acted in depth as buttress walls more than twelve feet wide on each side, and the roof was not pitched *upon* them but was built *into* them. In my earliest experimental drawings I had tried pitching the roof at an angle approaching 50°, for at first sight Hollar's pictures seem to indicate the steep angle one might expect. But it turned out not to be so. Working throughout on the principle that results must imitate Hollar's pictures as closely as possible, it was not until I had reduced the roof angle to 45° that I was able to produce a result, at Hollar's perspective, which gave a roof of his proportion in relation to the rest of the building. All others were too steep, too high, and too heavy. It would appear that the builders were anxious to reduce the height, and with it the increased mass and weight of a steeper pitch, and were able to do so because of the exceptional width of the containing walls—i.e. the gallery frame—in this special instance.

At its widest span, where the frontal wall of the roof acts as a frame across the diameter, it thrusts against and into the existing framework at the midway angles of the encircling galleries. For this reason, as will be seen from the plan at fig. 22, the centre line is set across to the corners of the galleries, and not to the centres of the bays.[1] The effect of this on an even-numbered polygon is that the centre of the tiring-house area also faces a corner, and not the flat or centre of a bay. This is contrary to the practice of all reconstructions hitherto; but that the building was indeed laid out in this way seems to be confirmed not only by the structural economy and logic of the bearing of the roof frontal, but

[1] All plan and elevation drawings given here are reproduced to the scale of 1/16th inch to 1 foot, and rough measurements may therefore be taken from them. But it is to be understood that they are freehand diagrams for purposes of explanation only, and not architectural drawings in the technical sense of that term. Because of this it will be found that they are not everywhere consistent in all their details. Consider them as work in progress, or variations upon a theme still capable of further variation. What matters here is the theme.

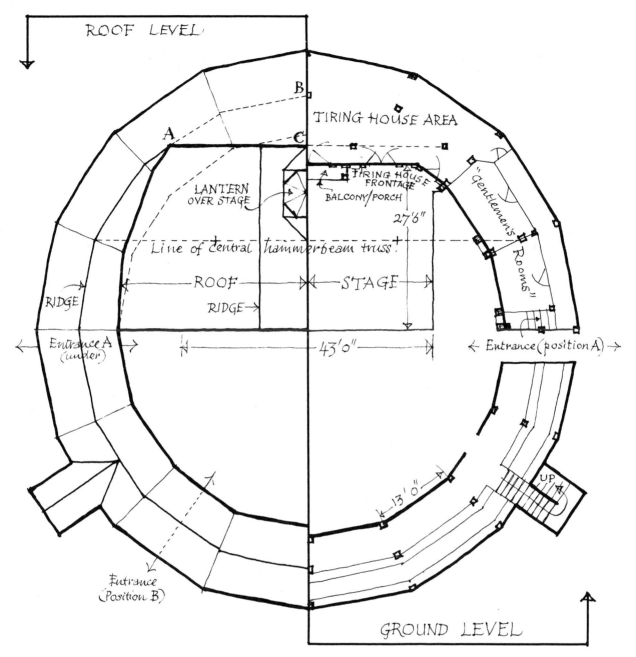

ROOF LEVEL

B

A C

TIRING HOUSE AREA

LANTERN
OVER STAGE

TIRING HOUSE
FRONTAGE
BALCONY/PORCH

27'6"

"Gentlemen's
Rooms"

Line of central hammerbeam truss

RIDGE

ROOF RIDGE → STAGE

Entrance A
(under)

43'0"

← Entrance (position A) →

13'0"

UP

Entrance
(Position B)

GROUND LEVEL

22. *Overall dimensions: plan*

by another circumstance which presented itself spontaneously
as a result of this deduction, and is to be shown later.

Having set the roof frontal across the diameter and pitched
it at an angle of 45°, I now offer a sketch of it as fig. 23.
It is to be noted in Hollar's etching that upon this frontal he
has clearly indicated the timber framing, which he shows nowhere else in the building, nor even at the nearby Hope, which

63

we know for certain was timber-framed. It may perhaps be assumed that by the time Hollar saw them these buildings had been faced all over with plaster, like so many of the houses he shows in the Long View which have every indication in other respects of being timber-framed. The practice of rendering over timber with plaster or cement became common in London during the seventeenth century.[1] Assuming that the Globe was treated so, I also assume that this rendering was omitted from the roof frontal to avoid needlessly increasing the suspended weight of it.

My sketch of the frontal shows a system of framing which is balanced to support itself by the pressure of its own weight upon the centre and upon the points at each end where it is locked into the framework of the main building. Two long bracing-pieces springing from the floor level of the topmost gallery serve to reduce the unsupported span at the centre and give something of the appearance of a shallow arch. Shadowy indications on the etching suggest a pair of windows, and these I have therefore included. A horizontal member across the frontal above the window line, on a level with the ridge of the gallery roof, is clearly indicated in the etching and strongly emphasized in Hollar's drawing. This in my reconstruction is the front member of the (on plan) rectangular frame which carries the major weight of the roof. Thus only a small part of the frontal below it needs to support itself across the centre span. Note how the whole frontal is braced diagonally to prevent its collapsing into the centre.

[1] See Irwin Smith, *Shakespeare's Globe Playhouse*, 1956, p. 45n.

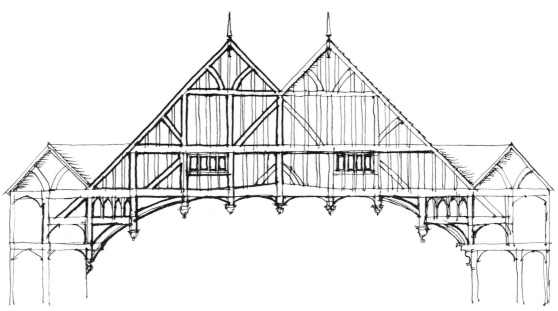

23. Superstructure: frontal screen

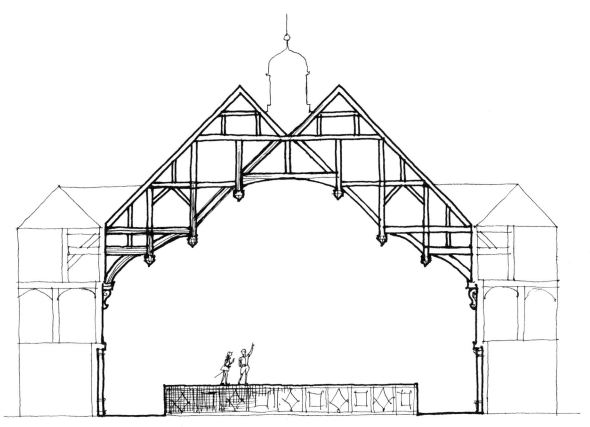

24. Superstructure: central truss

A similar frame would be erected at the rear of the superstructure. Between the two I am supposing there would have
been a central truss, perhaps on a system of hammer beams such
as is shown at fig. 24. It might indeed have been simpler than this,
but if so it would have entailed the use of larger timbers, which I
have tried to avoid. The longest timbers in the central truss as
shown here are 16 feet. Sixteen feet is also the depth of each of
the two sections of the roof from front to rear, as divided by the
central truss. It will be seen from the plan, as well as from the side
elevation of the building (fig. 25), that the roof, fore and aft,
measures only half its breadth across the centre. The effect from
this side viewpoint is rather surprising. Nevertheless it conforms
closely to the proportion and general appearance, in relation to
the rest of the building, shown in both Hollar's etching and his
sketch. Fig. 26, which presents a perspective of the Globe
according to the dimensions given here, and viewed from approximately the position of the Hollar pictures, may now be compared
with these. When allowance is made for the trees and houses
which hide the bottom part of the building in Hollar, and

65

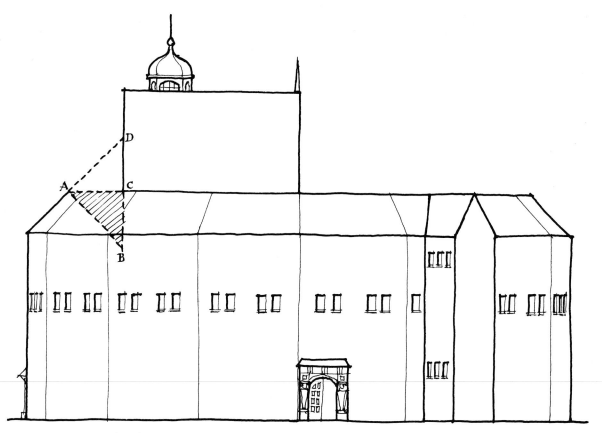

25. *Exterior: side elevation, indicating alternative treatments at rear of superstructure*

remembering the differences we have found in his two versions, between which we have to steer a course, it must surely be granted that the effect is very close to these and so, presumably, to their original.[1]

At first, when I had arrived at this point I thought it unnecessary to go further; but then, if only for the satisfaction of completeness, I decided I ought to try to imagine a view of the building from the back, the dark side of this moon as it were, which Hollar does not show. The result surprised me.

The problem involved may be seen on the plan (fig. 22) and in the side elevation (fig. 25). The back side of the superstructure roof is set on to the building in a straight line across a chord of the surrounding circle. If there are other ways of setting it out

[1] In this and the following exterior sketches I have shown up the polygonal anatomy of the building by emphasizing rather strongly the shadows at the turn of the walls. In reality, except in certain conditions of strong sunlight, the angles of the walls and the roof would appear much less emphasized, and the whole building would tend to have a more rounded look than here.

they would be so purposelessly complicated that they need not
be considered. But this way, though simple in itself, leaves a
curving gap between the ridge of the surrounding roof and the
rear face of the superstructure. The area of the gap is shown in
the shaded portion in fig. 25, and on the plan (fig. 22) in the area
ABC. It is possible—and in an early drawing I explored the
possibility—that a part of this gap could have been filled by a
gabled hut or dormer projecting from the back of the superstructure; but I could offer no good reason for the extra com-
plication of doing this. In making the present reconstruction it
seemed to me that the marriage of a large rectangular-planned
timber roof to a large polygon of timber galleries was in itself such
a complicated task of carpentry that at all points where they had
any choice the carpenters would have been likely to adopt the

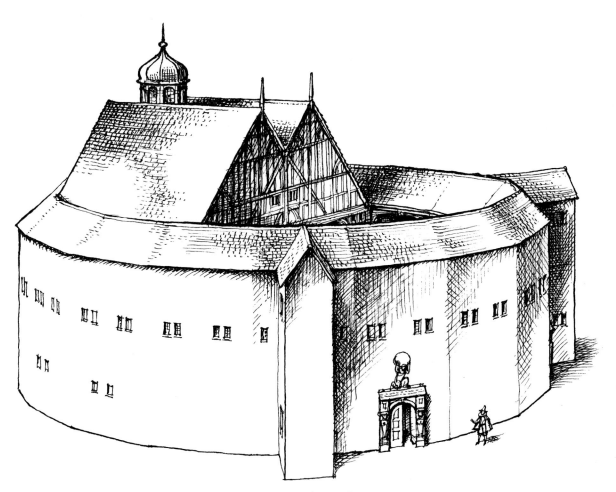

26. The Second Globe: reconstruction as seen from the Long View position

most simple and direct procedure available to them. Since in fig. 25 it is nonsensical to suppose that they would have continued round with the inner pitch of the gallery roof on the downward line AB (as a trap for rainwater), they were left with only two simple alternatives: to level off with a leaded roof on a line AC, or to continue their outside rafters upwards on the line AD to meet the back wall of the superstructure. Since the last was by far the simplest available solution I have assumed that this was the one adopted. In the perspective drawing at fig. 27 I show the visual effect of doing this.

It will be seen that as the roof ridge curves out away from the superstructure wall, its rafters reach further and further up the wall towards a peak at their farthest extent. Its architectural appearance is perhaps not very pleasing, and on that ground alone I was on the point of rejecting it after the first sketch, when at the same instant I saw it in a clear and unexpected light of familiar recognition. Its resemblance to the peaked-up shape of that curious roof at the nearby Hope playhouse was startling. It could not be disregarded. Further study with comparative drawings tended only to confirm my growing conviction that there was a fundamental relationship between the two structures. The argument is as follows:

Let it be supposed that at a theatre resembling the Globe and having a rear view such as we have seen in fig. 27, it became necessary for some reason to remove the superstructure. (There might be many reasons: the superstructure might have become unsafe, let us say through damage by fire; or it might simply have been found to make the place too dark.) The diagram at fig. 28 now shows the theatre, viewed from the same rear position as before but with its superstructure removed. On the inward side, however, the roof space, where the superstructure used to be, is now stripped open, and the rafters have lost their supporting wall. Next let it be supposed that the builders have been instructed to repair the roof and cover it in as quickly and cheaply as possible; that is to say, the proprietors do not wish to go to the expense of dismantling and rebuilding all that part of the roof merely for the aesthetic satisfaction of making it level with the rest of the circle: it is simply to be patched up safe and weatherproof, using material salvaged from the demolished superstructure, and that is all. The builders therefore have done no more than set up two

27. Reconstruction: rear view

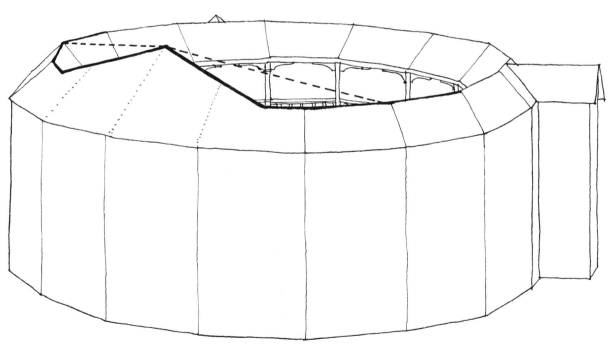

28. Rear view, with superstructure removed

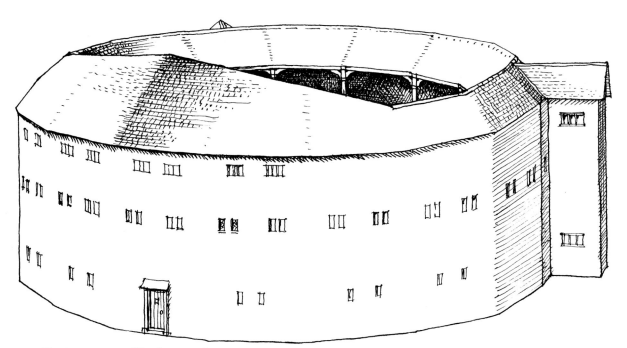

29. Playhouse modified: rear view

new ridge purlins across the opened-up area, extended the rafter line to meet it, and tiled it over. The dotted line on the diagram shows the area of this repair. The inward side below the new ridge, being now a vertical plane nearly all the way round, would have been treated as a wall surface, perhaps with openings. It could have been tile-hung, since all the material was ready to hand.

The effect when thus completed, seen from the rear position as before, is shown at fig. 29. A different view of the same thing, seen this time from the position from which Hollar drew and etched his view of the Hope, is given at fig. 30. It will be seen that the appearance of this new roof-line now imitates so exactly the strange outline of the Hope (or 'Globe') in Hollar, which has been perhaps one of the most mysterious of all the sphinx-like riddles surrounding the Globe ever since the Long View was published, that it is surely hard to doubt that here at last we have a satisfactory answer to it.

The history of the professional use of the Hope after its opening in 1614 may (in two different senses) help to throw some light upon the matter. Whatever Henslowe's and Meade's hope may have been for recapturing a share of the stage-play public on Bankside, it was short-lived. Only one important theatrical event ever took place at the Hope, the first performance of Jonson's

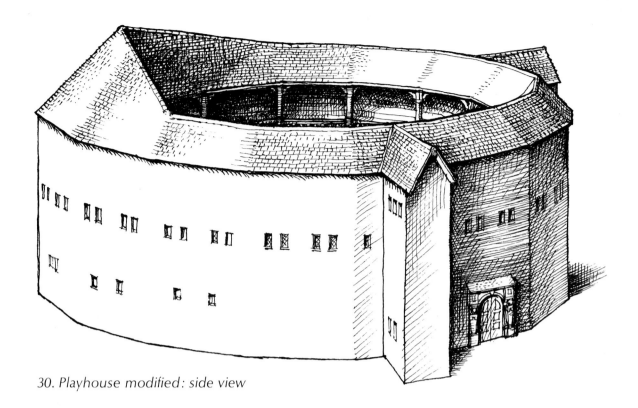

30. *Playhouse modified: side view*

Bartholomew Fair on 31 October 1614. Two separate companies, Lady Elizabeth's Men and Prince Charles's Men, occupied it in succession, for brief periods, but after three years both had left, and thereafter no company and nothing of dramatic interest is associated with it. The reason is clearly indicated by Professor Bentley.[1] 'Actors', he says, nicely, 'are not constituted to accommodate graciously to the competition of bears.' The original dual-purpose intention of the Hope, as playhouse and baiting-house, did not work. The actors soon and strongly objected to the limitations and inconveniences imposed on them by the bear-baiting side of the business which continued at all events to be the chief public attraction of the house.[2] Henslowe died in 1616, and thereafter his partner Meade concentrated more and more on animal-baiting. By the time Hollar came to London it would seem that even the playhouse name of the Hope had ceased to be commonly used, it being then simply known as the bear-baiting house. And perhaps before he arrived, certainly before he made his drawing, 'the Heavens' which had been built 'all over' the portable stage had been dismantled. Without plays the

---

[1] G. E. Bentley, *The Jacobean and Caroline Stage*, vol. 6, pp. 200–14.
[2] According to Ben Jonson the Hope, only a few months after its opening, was 'as filthy as Smithfield, and as stinking every whit'. (*Bartholomew Fair*, Prologue.)

Heavens served no purpose, and for bear-baiting purposes they robbed the arena of too much light. This question of light we shall refer to again in another chapter, but it is certain that the large half-way roof over an arena narrower than the Globe's, as the Hope's seems to have been, and without the Globe's provision of windows (as may also be seen in the etching), the daylight must have been much obscured.

But in this comparison between the Globe and the Hope the chief point has now to be made. If it is true, as I have demonstrated, that the Heavens superstructure at the Hope was dismantled, and that in its original form it resembled the one we see at the Globe, it must now be recalled that we know from the evidence of the contract that the Heavens at the Hope was designed 'to be borne or carried without any posts or supporters to be fixed or set upon the said stage'. That being so, it strongly corroborates the conclusion already reached from other reasoning, that the Heavens at the Globe was likewise borne or carried without the support of posts upon the stage.

Two final points should be mentioned in this connection. The first is that in my earliest experimental sketches, wherein I first noticed the resemblance between the humped-up back roofs at the Globe and the Hope, I was working with the polygonal plan set out, as always previously, with its stage front parallel with one of the bays of the polygon, and not to a corner as here. Though the exterior shape was still familiar it did not then come up to the sharp peak which Hollar shows. I supposed at that time that he had derived the effect from a trick of perspective, seeing the top edge of the roof sideways on. But when later I had reset the roof structure, in a different relation to the polygon (for the purpose only of lining up the roof frontal with the corner framing of the galleries), the relative re-positioning of the corners at once and of itself produced Hollar's peaked effect at the back. I take this, therefore, as corroboration for this way of laying out the plan.

The second point is that if the argument given in this chapter is correct, Hollar's accidental reversing of the names of 'The Globe' and the 'Beere baytinge h(ouse)' is in one sense a less significant confusion than it appears to be; at least, if he had taken his view only a few years previously, the two buildings would have looked so alike as to have made very little difference.

7

The Lantern

Between the two roofs of the superstructure stands that feature which Professor Bentley, referring to the Long View version, describes as 'an odd onion-shaped tower unique in pictures of early London theatres, and of unknown function'.[1] It is indeed rather odd, but Bentley is surely right to imply that although 'of unknown function', a function of some sort it must have had. If it had none it could only have been erected as a decoration, and it may be doubted whether any builder in his right mind would have put up such an expensive decorative feature in a position where from ground level it could hardly be seen, and from nowhere to any advantage. As for the onion shape, it is certainly not an English style, in the bulbous form it has in the etching. Hollar would have seen such shapes in his youth in Bohemia, and in Antwerp where, as we have seen, he was living at the time he made the etching; the style of it may therefore have been partly influenced by reflexes from his background. The cupola does not have the same bulbous appearance in Hollar's original drawing, where it is shown with a more typically English Tudor turret-cap or 'point'.

In other pictures of Elizabethan theatres, turrets of a kind are usually shown flying the playhouse flag, and it may be assumed that this was what they were chiefly built for. The business of hoisting the flag to a position where it could be clearly seen from a distance was, after all, an important daily operation, to attract audiences. But it does not look as if the cupola at the Second Globe can have been meant for that purpose. There is no flagpole shown there—nor indeed, it must be admitted, anywhere else about the building, unless the vertical object above the farther staircase in the sketch may be taken for one. We may be sure there must have been a flagpole at the Globe, and it must have

---

[1] *The Jacobean and Caroline Stage*, vol. 6, p. 185.

73

been conspicuously placed and easy to reach once or twice every day. But a valley between two roofs is not the best place to pitch a flagpole, where other choices exist; and to erect an elaborate octagonal cupola would surely be a needlessly expensive way of giving access to such a flagpole if that is all the cupola was built to do. We ought therefore to ask what other purpose there might be for putting up a structure of this kind. We shall not have far to look for an answer. In medieval and renaissance buildings an octagonal turret placed midway upon a roof is either a louvre for ventilation or a lantern to let in light. The first would hardly seem to be needed in the present case; but the second would serve a particular need so well and so aptly in the position shown that I feel there can be little doubt that the cupola was in fact a lantern, set up to give additional daylight to the interior of the roof, the rear areas of the stage, and the façade of the tiring-house.

The problem of covering the open yard to provide maximum shelter without at the same time depriving the stage of light has already been referred to. In the public theatres this problem seems never to have been satisfactorily solved. John Webster complains in his introduction to the 1612 edition of *The White Devil* that 'it was acted in so dull a time of winter, and presented in so open and black a theatre that it wanted . . . a full and understanding auditory'. Thus we find a public theatre could indeed be open and 'black' at the same time, certainly in the dark days of winter. Henslowe's contract for the Fortune calls the roof over its stage a 'shadow'; and we have already noted there is reason to think the roof over the Hope may eventually have been dismantled because it obstructed the light. The big superstructure at the Second Globe would certainly have darkened the interior of the house a great deal unless something were done to restore the light it took, even assuming, as has been done in this reconstruction, that the Heavens was lifted as high as possible, to let in the light under its forward edge. Even so, it is likely the stage would have needed more light. Now it is to be seen in Hollar that the Globe was encircled with a continuous row of windows set at the height of the middle gallery. One may wonder what these windows were for, since the galleries were all open on the side giving on to the yard, and could themselves have had no need for them. But at the middle level such windows might very well

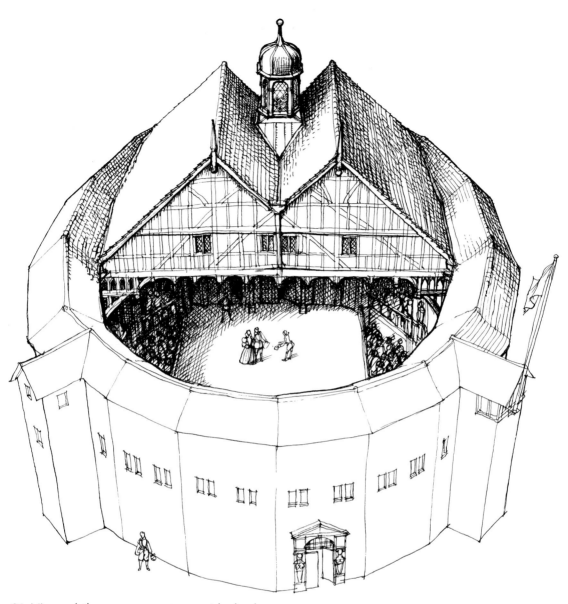

31. View of the superstructure with the lantern

have served to help light the whole interior.[1] It may be noted that the Hope does not appear to have had these windows, and so, with the additional fact that its yard seems to have been of narrower proportions, its superstructure must have made it a darker theatre, adding further likelihood to the supposition that

[1] Dr. Richard Southern, who was the first to draw attention to the problem of these windows, offered as a solution that they must have been needed to light a corridor around the back of the gallery, which gave access to a circle of closed-off 'rooms', rather like boxes at an opera house. But I have come to think the solution I offer here is more likely.

its superstructure was removed because of the need for more light.

So we return to the question of the lantern. Placed where it was, midway between the roofs and rather far to the rear, a large lantern eight feet across (as we have it here) and glazed all round would have thrown light directly upon the rear of the stage where it was most needed. It can be argued that if the Heavens roof-space had been closed in, say with a suspended painted cloth (if with nothing more solid), the lantern would then have been needed to light the roof-space itself. But it surely could not have been built for that purpose alone, for if so—supposing for example the roof *had* been closed in by a solid ceiling over the stage, supported no matter how—there would have been no need at all to build a lantern. The roof-space could and would then have been lit, with far less trouble and expense, simply by windows in the gable-ends, front or rear. Therefore the very presence of a lantern in that position does itself suggest the intention to throw a downward light on to the stage, and that in its turn tends to confirm that there was not any permanent obstruction such as a ceiling between the lantern and the stage below.

8

Notes on the Interior

Although it is not within the scope of this book to discuss the uses or methods of the Jacobean stage in any detail, it is nevertheless necessary at this point to show how the building which has here been reconstructed from Hollar's evidence would have accommodated the physical features of the Jacobean stage and its adjuncts, as they have now emerged from a consensus of opinion.[1] In outline, these features will, I think, be generally accepted as follows:

A broad stage of rectangular character projects from the rear wall where the backstage 'tiring-house' is, into the yard as far as the centre, the audience surrounding it on three sides. Giving on to the stage from the tiring-house are a number of doors of which one or two at least must be high and wide enough to allow the handling-through of fairly large objects such as beds, thrones, and chariots, and certain scenic pieces such as tombs or tents which might have to be erected on the stage. There must also be some provision for a curtained space within which simple tableaux can be arranged, to be revealed by drawing away the curtain. At an upper level there has to be an area which may be used occasion-

[1] It is a peculiar quality of this subject that it appears to be as absorbing to the general reader as to scholars, and I have tried in this book to make the matter acceptable to both, which I have not found easy. For example, at this point I would not wish the general reader, perhaps a newcomer to the subject, to feel himself fobbed off with only a brief nod towards the central matter of the subject, which is the use and management of the stage. But the canonical works are readily available. I need mention only *The Elizabethan Stage* (4 vols.) by Sir Edmund Chambers, with its continuation *The Jacobean and Caroline Stage* (7 vols.) by Gerald Eades Bentley. Glynne Wickham's *Early English Stages*, a comprehensive analytical work still in progress (its fourth and final part has yet to appear), will be found most useful and contains an invaluable up-to-date bibliography. I mention my own book *The Globe Restored* in this company not as comparable but because it gives a brief and illustrated outline from my own point of view, and is besides, though independent, in effect a companion to the present volume.

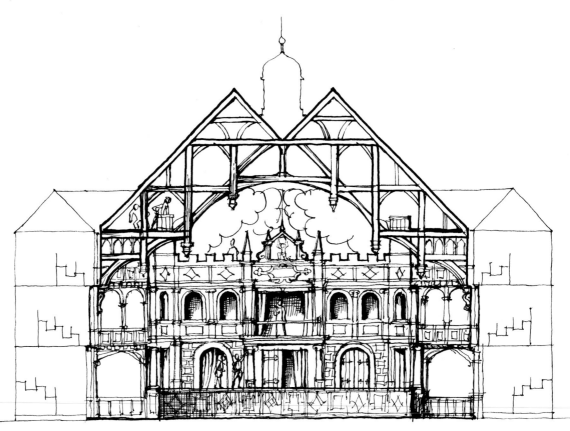

32. Section showing an arrangement for the tiring-house frontage

ally as an 'upper stage', big enough to accommodate several
actors, and fairly easily accessible from the main stage below. This
provides for such localities as Juliet's bedroom or Cleopatra's
monument. Additionally at this level there may be a number of
window openings. Higher up in the roof or ceiling of 'the Heavens'
there must be provision for the miraculous and splendid appear-
ances of divinities, and for flying them down towards the stage on
'cloud-borne' thrones or on the back of eagles (as in *Cymbeline*).
There is no dispute about the need for these arrangements, only
about their style, and the frequency and method of their use.
For present purposes, therefore, I have assembled my ideas about
how these things would have been adjusted to the circumstances
of the Second Globe in the drawing on pp. 90–1, and this
chapter will be set out in the form of notes explaining the considerations which have guided me in making this particular
interpretation.

The Stage. We have the plan dimensions of one Elizabethan
stage, that of the Fortune playhouse of 1600. It was 43 feet wide
by $27\frac{1}{2}$ feet deep, 'to the middle of the yard'. This is a very large

stage area by any ordinary standards, and has usually been found too large for adoption in reconstructions of a round-style public theatre (the Fortune of course was square). This follows from the usual and surely reasonable practice of basing reconstructions upon the dimensional guide-lines provided by Henslowe's Fortune and Hope contracts, so that the overall width of the yard is governed by the 55 feet width at the Fortune. But of course if that is made the diameter of a round yard, instead of the lateral dimension of a square, the area enclosed is reduced to such a degree that it is true the Fortune stage could not fit into it and still produce the style and proportion of an Elizabethan stage, such as from the evidence we believe these to have been. No harm therefore to reduce this over-large stage to the point where it can produce the right effect. However, here at the Second Globe we find a different situation. We have adopted a different form of control, based upon the Hollar pictures, and working from this direction we have found ourselves inescapably provided with a yard of much wider diameter than has been usual in recon- structions of round-style theatres. Into this wider yard the proportions of the Fortune stage now fit so well that it would seem an obtuse refusal of a gift of Providence, a snub to seren- dipity, not to adopt them as they stand. The diagram, fig. 33, shows the known dimensions of the Fortune and the estimated dimensions of the Second Globe overlaid in the same scale for comparison. In the diagram they are sharing the same stage, but I would emphasize that this convenient and interesting coincidence was not a factor, indeed was not ever considered, in the esti- mation of the Second Globe's circumference.

I have settled upon a stage height (from the ground) of 5 feet 6 inches. My reasons for assuming a high stage are given elsewhere.[1] This height would allow movement under the stage for, say, the working of a stage trap, though it would be somewhat crouching and uncomfortable. If the marshy ground upon which the Globe was built would allow another foot or even only a few inches of excavation it would provide a useful supplement of headroom. The stage of course might be built up higher still, but I have tried to avoid recourse to extreme situations.

There is reason to think that the stages of the First Globe and some other earlier theatres were not covered in all round with a

[1] See The Globe Restored, chap. 3.

frontal of boards, but were hung with cloth. At the Fortune, however, the stage was boarded in.[1] I have here assumed that with the advance of theatre building the Second Globe would have had a stage permanently boarded in below. If so, there

[1] So, it would seem, was the stage at the Boar's Head, an inn-yard theatre the history of which has recently been brought to light by Professor Herbert Berry. When the stage at the Boar's Head was taken down on one occasion, for rebuilding in another position, a great deal of rubbish was found underneath it, and a man had to be paid to clear it away. This suggests that it had been a closed-in space.

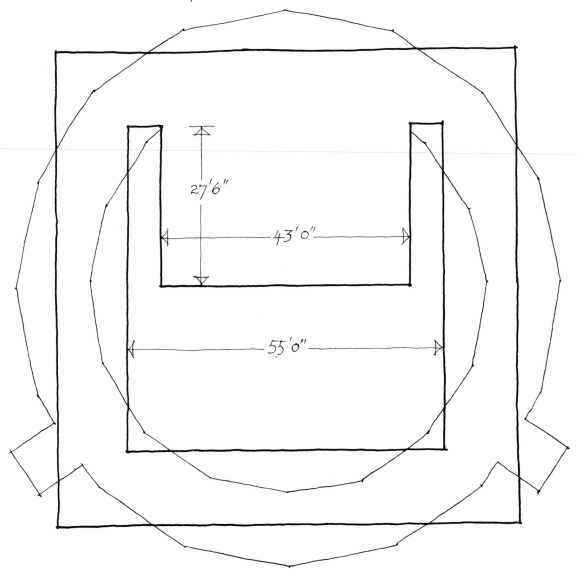

33. Comparative ground plans of the Fortune (dimensions known) and the Second Globe

should have been some means of lighting and and ventilating it. We are obliged to wonder whether there would not have been some openings made for this purpose.

   Style and Arrangement of the Tiring-House Façade. Thirty-seven years of successful professional experience had passed between the building of the first London playhouse and the rebuilding of the Globe. More than ten different playhouses had been constructed in that time, and it is not to be supposed that they were all left completely undecorated. Contemporary comment suggests that they *were* decorated, and we have no reason to suppose that the London theatres were either ignorant of, or had any reason for refusing to adopt, a style of bravura ornamentation that was universally employed by settled and sophisticated theatrical enterprises elsewhere, and was certainly available, technically, in London. The only reasons we could have for supposing they did not adopt it would be that they did not consider it dramaturgically suitable, which is unlikely, or that they could not afford it, which is untrue. Eighteen years before the Second Globe was built the interior of the Swan was described as having been painted to resemble marble; and sixteen years after, the *frons scenae* at the Cockpit was being designed by Inigo Jones as a fully-fashioned classical façade. In between there is plentiful evidence of spectacular scenic requirements on London stages, and of the flourishing of a sumptuous style of temporary painted architecture (such as was used for the festival arches for James I's coronation). I have therefore borrowed elements from all these effects to decorate the tiring-house façade of the Second Globe. The effect of battlements and painted stone masonry appears in several of the coronation arches, in scenic designs by Inigo Jones, and in the contemporary representation of a theatre by Robert Fludd.[1] It is a feature suggested as being a hangover from a traditional practice, and from the needs of those plays of an earlier taste (e.g. the three parts of *Henry VI*) in which the tiring-house is used for a besieged town and assaults are made upon its 'walls'.

   Two details on this façade as I have drawn it seem to me very appropriate. They are a modelled figure of Atlas (or Hercules) bearing a globe upon his shoulders, and below him a tablet or

[1] See *The Globe Restored*, plate 18.

81

cartouche framing an inscription. Such figures and mottoes were so usual a feature of baroque festival architecture that one might almost characterize them as indispensable. They appear abundantly in Flemish and Italian theatrical prints, in the London coronation arches of 1603, and designs by Inigo Jones. There is a tradition transmitted through the eighteenth-century antiquarian William Oldys that the Globe displayed 'a figure of Hercules supporting the Globe, under which was written *Totus mundus agit histrionem*' (loosely translated, 'All the world's a stage'). This is usually thought to have referred to a painted sign outside the theatre, and there is a reference in Heywood's *The English Traveller* to a 'statue' of 'Dame Fortune' outside the Fortune playhouse which gives substance to the idea, by association. In some of my drawings here I have accordingly put an Atlas figure over the entrance, but I cannot refrain from thinking it equally if not more likely that this figure and the motto were displayed, in the characteristic fashion of the time, upon the *frons scenae*; and in that fashion also I show them here.

The famous sketch by de Witt of the Swan playhouse shows only two large double-doors opening from the tiring-house on to the stage. Few reconstructors content themselves with this. It is certain that in some theatres there were more doors than two, and in Jones's Cockpit design there are five openings in the classical style of Palladio's theatre at Vicenza. Having at the Second Globe a 43-foot wide expanse of façade to deal with, and having also the supposition that the design of that façade was developed not without some sort of educated guidance and sophistication, I have inclined to associate it more with Jones's Cockpit than with de Witt's Swan, and have accordingly given it five openings on to the stage. All are doors capable of being shut not so much for dramatic purposes as simply at night to keep the weather out and the property in the tiring-house dry and secure. The central double-door I have made large enough to allow the passage of fairly large properties and scenic pieces, and it is flanked by two round-headed doors like those at the Swan, also capable of being passed through by, say, a chariot or a throng of people. Projecting in front of the centre opening I have placed a shallow 'porch' which can be used for hanging curtains and hiding tableaux pieces for 'discoveries'. Such curtains could if needed be continued, in the layout I give here, right across the stage from

34. *A curved arrangement for the tiring-house frontage in a style partly suggested by Inigo Jones's designs for the Cockpit-in-Court. (The supposition of a cloud border as shown here hiding the hammerbeam truss, is perhaps carrying fancy too far, but it is at least worth the indulgence of a sketch.)*

side to side, in a manner that has been suggested by Richard Hosley.[1] The roof of the porch now serves as the floor of a small 'upper stage' at the level of the middle spectator gallery, with an opening at the back into the tiring-house, and this is flanked on each side by window openings. The whole of this range of openings forms a sort of passage closed off from the interior of the tiring-house by doors at each end. On the stage side they are hung with curtains.

[1] 'The Discovery-space in Shakespeare's Globe', *Shakespeare Survey 12*, 1959.

83

The arrangement described above can in fact fulfil the require-ments of most if not all Elizabethan play texts as related to their problems of staging, implicit or explicit. It has been designed to do so; it is therefore a synthesis; and it may therefore be faulted on that score alone. It is perhaps easier in this matter to provide a collective composition made up of arbitrary solutions to all the different problems, than to decide deliberately which of the problems to leave unsolved. But since it would be unreasonably difficult for me to have myself change an arrangement only because to me it looks too reasonably accommodating, I will leave it as it is, and so pass to the next question.

The Heavens. That this is the most unusual feature of this reconstruction must follow from the fact that it was specifically to try to find an explanation for its unusualness, as seen from the exterior, that has caused the whole reconstruction to be evolved. Most of its problems have therefore been dealt with in the earlier discussion of it as a roof structure. What remains is to consider how it was used theatrically.

The dramatic requirement was for a mechanical flying device, to lift and lower gods and heroes between earth and heaven, like Drusilla in her flying dragon-chariot in Massinger's *The Prophetess*, performed at the Globe in 1622, or Peter Pan of our own day, one of the most persistent popular tricks in theatre history, and one which was a constant pleasure to Elizabethan audiences. In the older Elizabethan theatres this seems to have been effected by a direct drop to the stage from a windlass situated overhead in the hut-like superstructure, as it is shown in the sketch of the Swan. It might have been done in this fashion at the Second Globe, but if so there would have had to be some sort of platform with a catwalk to it, built into the vaulting over the stage in a position which would certainly have interfered with the light from the lantern, even if it did not shut it out altogether. (It could be argued from this that the lantern itself was no lantern after all, but a cupola to house the windlass; but that is most unlikely, for such a cupola would at best have been very cramped for the purpose, and it would certainly not have been considered worth while to go to the extra expense of building an elaborate octagon where a rectangular hut would have served the purpose better.) It there-fore seems most likely that whatever the practice may have been

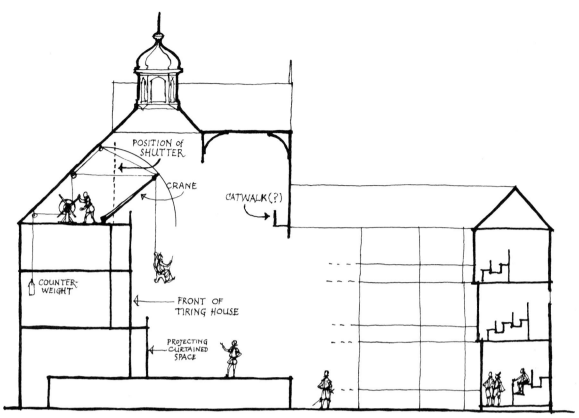

POSITION of
SHUTTER

CRANE

CATWALK(?)

COUNTER-
WEIGHT

FRONT OF
TIRING HOUSE

PROJECTING
CURTAINED
SPACE

35. Diagrammatic section showing relative positions of lantern, tiring-house, and Heavens

at other theatres, the classic flying effect at the Second Globe had
to be managed without a direct drop. There was, however,
another method available, as classic, if not more so, than the
first.

Accepting that the vault over the stage was left clear up to the
lantern, there still remained an excellent platform for the management of flying effects. This was the space over the top of the
tiring-house and under the big humped-up cowl of the roof at the
back. Here was room enough for drum, windlass, and cordage,
and for the actor to be prepared in his flying chair. The only
question was how to project him forward to a position from
which he could be descended to the stage. It was a question with
a ready answer. It needed only a simple crane, a jib-arm some
fourteen or fifteen feet long, hinged to the floor of the platform
and controlled by a rope-and-pulley system at the upper end.
From a cross-bar at that upper end the flying chair was suspended
by a pair of long lines, these running back through pulleys to a
drum and windlass. When the jib-arm was released it would
swing from its hinge forward and downward, through an arc of

85

some forty-five degrees, carrying the chair forward from the
tiring-house top until it hung over the stage. At the same time,
the windlass being released, under the braking control of a leather
strap around its axle, the lines carrying the chair would be
allowed to run out so that the chair would descend gently to the
stage. It would be balanced by a counterweight hung in the tiring-
house. With rehearsal the whole operation would be managed as
one movement, the chair and its occupier emerging from the top
of the tiring-house with first a slight upward motion to clear the
edge, then forward and downward towards the stage. It should be
noted that all this would take place directly under the lantern,
from which the light would fall directly upon the spectacle of the
descending god.

The mechanics of all this would be to some extent visible.
I have suggested in my drawing that the preparation would be
done behind a screen painted with clouds above the tiring-house,
and that when all was ready a pair of shutters would be opened in
the middle, to allow the forward emergence of the throne. This,
with its gilded dressing and its costumed actor, would tend to
attract the eye away from the jib and the ropes which suspended
it. But beyond that, the willing suspension of disbelief would have
to serve, as usual.

None of the machinery here described would have been
unfamiliar to the promoters of the Jacobean stage. The crane
device was known of old, and had been used in the theatres of
ancient Greece, as described by Pollux in Roman times. It was
described again with elaborate variations by Nicola Sabbatini in
Practica di fabricar scene e machine ne' teatri in 1638; and it was
not forgotten or unused in all the time between.[1] If the Globe
management had not known of such devices before, which is
very unlikely, they could have learned all they needed from Inigo
Jones, who had used a crane arrangement with cloud shutters in
Ben Jonson's masque *Hymenai* at Whitehall in 1606. Ben Jonson
himself had helped to operate the machines used in that masque.

It would be possible to run two galleries along under the roof,
one at each side, from the tiring-house top to the front frame.
I have indicated this in the drawings on pp. 78 and 90–1. These
again might be connected by a catwalk running along the inside

[1] Sabbatini gives a diagram, which is reproduced in Allardyce Nicoll, *Stuart
Masques and the Renaissance Stage*, 1937, p. 66.

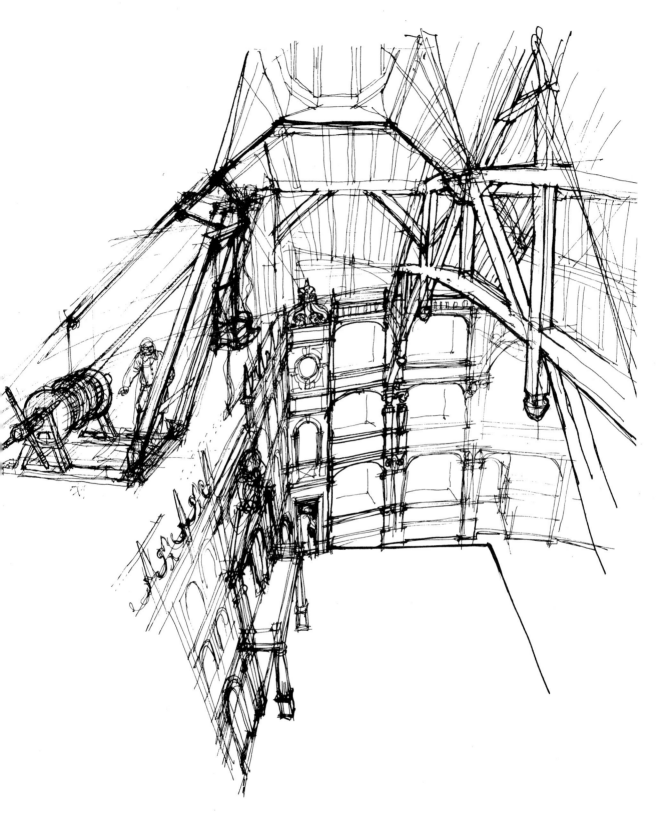

36. *A sketch in the Heavens*

of the frontal, as shown in fig. 35. With this, the whole space of the Heavens would begin to take on the appearance of the flies and fly-floor of a modern theatre. It would certainly provide a useful facility for the handling of special effects. But what might follow? I have been apt to consider the possibility of spreading star-painted blue canopies over the space from side to side, or of hanging sky borders and 'cloudings' in the Heavens. Such things were known about and done at that time; but not on such a large scale. The ceiling over the stage of Jones's Cockpit in 1630 was hung across with 'Callicoe' (presumably coloured blue), with 'a great number of Starre of Assidue' fastened to it by copper rings, all very fine. But that was a small theatre, with only half the Heavens area of the vaulted space over the Globe. When the Globe is rebuilt will be the right time to decide what might or might not have been done there, in just such particulars as this.

Public Doors and Standings. John Chamberlain, writing to his friend Sir Ralph Winwood about the burning of the First Globe, said that 'it was a great marvaile and fair grace of God, that the people [in the theatre] had so little harm, having but two narrow doors to get out'. In 1643 the newspaper *The Weekly Account*, reporting a raid made by the authorities on the Fortune playhouse during a prohibited performance, says that 'there was set a strong guard of Pikes and muskets on both gates of the Playhouse'. Much earlier, in 1592, Henslowe, in his account of expenses for renovations at the Rose playhouse on Bankside, mentioned 'makeing the penthowsse shed at the tyeringe howsse doore'. Given these facts, it is for conjecture to decide whether the 'two narrow doors' and 'both gates' in the first two instances included or excluded 'the tyeringe howsse doore' (assuming there was a separate one, which there need not have been) at these theatres.

Conventional reconstruction has always assumed a single public entrance centrally placed directly opposite the stage, with a tiring-house door at the back. A view showing the Curtain playhouse in Shoreditch, drawn about 1600, which is the only view showing a door at all, seems to confirm this arrangement. Nevertheless I am not myself at all easy in my mind about such an arrangement, especially at the Second Globe. Would a large theatre, which we are assured held audiences of three thousand persons, have been built with only one public door, especially after the management's recent experience of a calamitous fire? I am inclined to think there would have been two public gates, with a tiring-house door in addition.

Supposing, however, that at the Second Globe there was only one public gate, it is unlikely in the terms of the present reconstruction to have been centrally placed opposite the stage, because, as we have seen, the polygonal frame necessarily places one of the angles of the polygon in that position. The gate would therefore have to be placed off-centre. That is no great matter, except perhaps for people of an inflexibly symmetrical disposition of mind. Being rather of that mind myself, and having by my choice two gateways into the auditorium to dispose of, my inclination is to balance them symmetrically. I find two positions available, and have indicated them variously (without making a final decision) in various of my drawings here. On the plan (p. 63) they are shown as entrance positions A and B. The logic of a designer would I think recommend position A. The entrances there lie off to the side in a comparatively 'dead' area of the auditorium's circumference. They are well separated for the crowds to disperse on leaving, and are in fact in the classical position of entrances to Greek and Roman theatres. Most importantly, they leave an uninterrupted arc of gallery-space available for the audience in the best position facing the stage. On the other hand they are badly placed in relation to the approach road, Maid Lane, which led directly past the Globe on its north side, which was also the direction leading from the landing-stages at the riverside. Would it not be a psychological mistake to oblige the playhouse patrons to leave the road and walk round to entrances at the side, almost hidden from the road, behind the staircases? I think in the end I should be obliged to conclude that there must have been one entrance at least as near as possible to and visible from Maid Lane.

This chapter has now begun to lengthen itself with incidentals which lie beyond the particular purpose of this work. Nevertheless, a point remains to be made about the use of the lowermost gallery. How much of this gallery space, if any, was arranged for seating? It is usually supposed that all of it, in all theatres, would have been provided with benches. If so, there had to be an arrangement whereby the heads of all those seated spectators would be higher than the people standing in front of them in the

37. The Second Globe: a reconstruction of the interior

yard. Either the yard would have to be dug down a little, or the scaffolds for seating in the bottom gallery would have to be built up. The first I think would be avoided on the marshy ground of the Bankside site. But before we accept the second we should pause to ask whether the lowest gallery was not at least partly a standing place, like the yard, but with the benefit of being under cover. Three references come to mind. In 1597 there was an injunction issued against the Burbages and their associates at the Theatre and the Curtain in Shoreditch, bidding them 'plucke down quite the stages, gallories and roomes that are made for people to stand in'; and a very early reference (1576) in Lambard's *Perambulation of Kent* mentions the fact that people who go to a 'common place, to behold Beare bayting, Enterludes, or Fence playe', must 'first paye one penny at the gate, another at the entrie of the Scaffolde, and third for a quiet standing'. Thirdly, there is a well-known account by a Swiss doctor, Thomas Platter, writing of his visits to the London playhouses in 1599, who says: 'The places are so built that they play on a raised platform and every one can well see it all. There are, however, separate galleries *and there one stands more comfortably* [my italics], and moreover can sit, but one pays more for it.' At the Hope, when the stage was removed and the house turned over to its alternative employment as a bull- and bear-baiting arena, were the patrons in the lowermost gallery seated or standing? It would seem more in the nature of such a place to have a crowd of standing spectators, and there would be room for a larger crowd that way. Hesitating, therefore, with these ideas in mind, I compromised, and have here arranged for the bottom gallery at the Second Globe to have a six-foot passageway to allow for standing in front, with two rows of benches raised above them at the back.

Lastly, on pages 96 and 97 below, it will be found that I have inserted a number of my sketch-book drawings and notes. Their purpose is simply to act as a demonstration of present flexibility, and a prophylactic against the premature hardening-out of enthusiastic ideas.

9

Reconstruction in Use

Such, then, are the outlines of the building that could be erected to represent as closely as possible the character of that English public playhouse of the beginning of the seventeenth century, the Globe, which was the workshop of Shakespeare and his companions. For our model we have chosen Hollar's picture of the Second Globe, believing, as has been demonstrated, that Hollar is a reliable witness, and that by accepting what he tells us we can keep our subject clearly in view without the smudgings of an unacceptable degree of conjecture. Conjectures there have been and must still be, but in this study and up to this point I would claim that the arguments are—or at least to me they seem— unavoidable, logical conclusions separately adduced from premises clearly exposed in primary evidence. What has emerged in general has come largely as a surprise to me; it is not the sort of thing I originally set out to find. Since it has produced itself, therefore, I must consider that it will to some extent justify itself. At least it may be observed, and I take it to be a sort of virtue, that although separate deductions have sometimes been used to help corroborate each other, they are not essentially inter-dependent. To remove any single part of the argument will not tumble the rest.

If it seems a pity to lose the thatched roof and the twin posts so familiar in reconstructions of the First Globe and other earlier playhouses, the loss nevertheless brings with it some compen-sating advantages for a reconstruction intended to be useful as well as historically interesting in the modern world. The simple, clear semi-circle of open space above the yard at the Second Globe allows much more readily for the setting up of a roof over it, without the ugliness and difficulty which would be encountered if one were to try to do it at a theatre of the earlier type, with the overhead hut projecting as shown in the Swan drawing. Here again the fact of its having a tiled roof, and not thatch, is helpful.

93

Shakespeare's Second Globe

I have elsewhere written strongly against the proposition of roofing-over the yard, and I do not wish here to upset that opinion in principle, since openness to weather and to the daylight from above is perhaps the most characteristic of all the famous features of this famous playhouse. Even so, however reluctantly, it has to be conceded by a reasonable man that for such a building to be fully useful nowadays it might indeed be preferable to keep the wind and weather out, let alone the noise of traffic. That ought not to mean, however, that the sky above the yard would not still be the principal source of light. The new roof, which should be laid into the building without disturbance to its original form, ought to be constructed of translucent material, preferably of transparent glass (double-glazed for warmth and to avoid condensation) through which the upper parts of the gabled frontage might still be seen by those in the yard below. Such a roof could be set up at a shallow pitch against the gable frontage in such a way that little if anything of it would be seen from outside the building. In a city site there would have to be ready access and means laid on to keep it washed down. It will be noted that the tiled roof of the Second Globe, which allows the use of gutters, makes this practicable, as the thatch of the earlier theatre would not have done.[1] Lastly in this connection, the Second Globe's banishment of the two great stage posts, however much lamented for their picturesqueness, would certainly render the unencumbered stage more generally useful for the needs of a modern auditorium.

The word 'useful', which occurred twice in the last paragraph, brings in the question which we ought now to consider: having erected such a building as this, what would be the use of it? Implicit in this question is of course the possibility or otherwise of

[1] If this Globe were to be built in a country or parkland setting, which would in many ways be preferable to any other, and if it were planned chiefly for summer use without heating, as an open-air theatre or exhibit, there might be no need for a fixed roof, though there would still be need for protection against inclement weather. For this purpose there could be a simple and indeed very attractive provision: a large tent or velarium of white translucent nylon, a 'big top' whose attachments would be built-in to the surrounding roof, which could be hoisted into position over the yard whenever needed, and in that position drawn open or closed at will from the top gallery. Once again the tiled roof, with gutters, makes this practicable.

commercial profit. One aspect of this large matter ought here to be stated clearly. In nearly every case where the rebuilding of the Globe has been proposed by practical men, often but not always actors or men of the theatre, the proposal has been to build and use it as a commercially viable *theatre*—that is, a place designed primarily for the production of plays. In my opinion such an approach to the problem is ill-judged, unpractical, and doomed to failure from the start. For if one should build an historically useful and proper reconstruction of a Jacobean playhouse, even supposing it were built of such strong and fire-resistant materials as would satisfy the public licensing authorities (which could be done), by the time one had complied with all the other necessary regulations which are imposed by those authorities for the safe arrangement of a theatre—spacing of seats, width of aisles and corridors, disposal of exits, etc.—the audience capacity would be likely to be reduced to a level well below that which commercial theatre managements usually consider worth their while. It has also to be borne in mind that a performance of a Shakespeare play in a Jacobean theatre, under 'true' Jacobean circumstances and with those certain truly Jacobean discomforts and lacks of facility which would be entailed, though it would be a truly interesting and, doubtless, rewarding experience for all the spectators there, these would, when they had had it once, have had it for good. They would like it and they would recommend it to others, but they would not themselves feel any urgent compulsion to go back. Thereafter they would go as before to more comfortable modern theatres. But if to avoid all these commercial disadvantages one were to increase the audience capacity, provide comfortable seats with good sight-lines, install various modern easements and facilities, and comply with normal safety regulations; and if one were then to provide the sophisticated equipment for modern play-production techniques, which would enable this supposed Jacobean theatre to be used in a flexible and commercially viable manner for modern needs, one would then have not a Jacobean playhouse at all, or anything remotely like it (except for one single though admittedly important characteristic, the thrust-out 'apron' stage): one would have in fact what we have already, thanks to the moving spirit and imagination of the late Sir Tyrone Guthrie, an excellent modern theatre specializing in open-style productions, as at Stratford, Ontario; at Minneapolis;

95

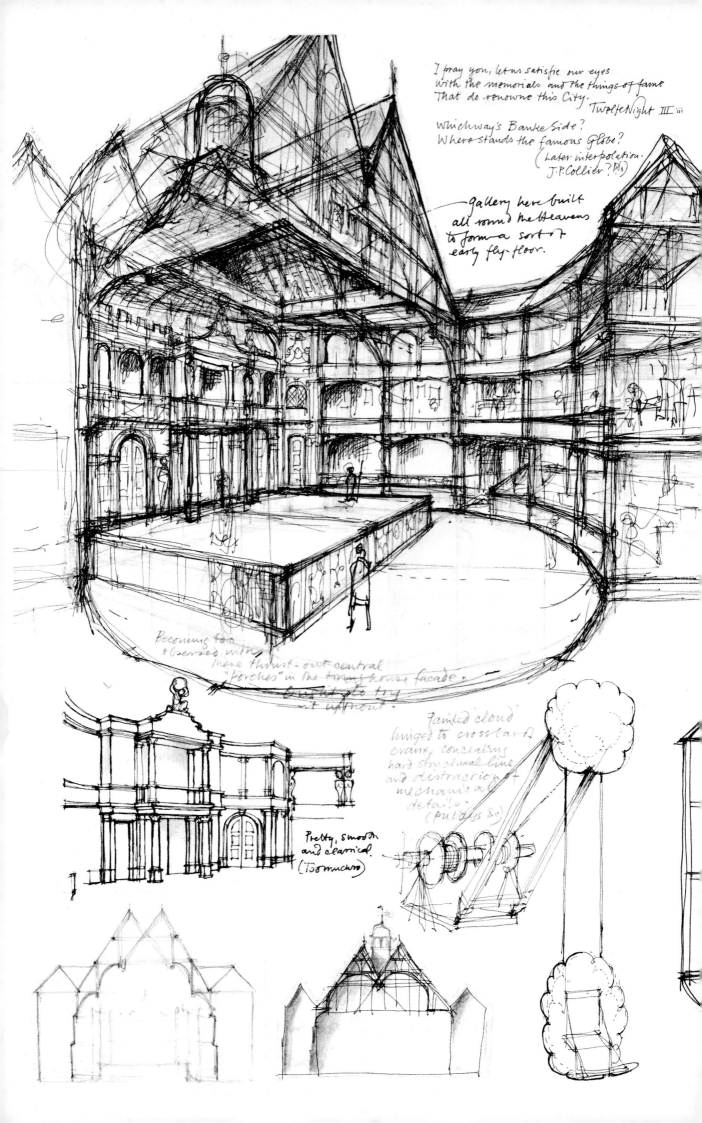

I pray you, let us satisfie our eyes
With the memorials and the things of fame
That do renowne this City. *Twelfe Night III.iii*

Whichway's Banke Side?
Where stands the famous Globe?
(Later interpolation.
J.P. Collier? 1801)

→ gallery here built
all round the Heavens
to form a sort of
early fly-floor.

Becoming too
obsessed with
these thrust-out central
"porches" in the tiring house facade.
Ought to try
it without.

Painted 'cloud'
hinged to crossband
crane, concealing
hard structural line
and distraction of
mechanical
details.
(pulleys &c)

Pretty, smooth
and classical.
(Too much so)

'Fly floor' opening lining
with cloud borders
(?)

Heavens here partly
supported on corbels
or brackets springing
from the gallery — is
all too much?

Wedge-shaped stage
à la Roxana Robs
but I think
otherwise rather
less than am
likely

Glass roof
over yard ?

...thing will ever
accomplished
all possible
...ections must...
...t be overcome.
...son
Rasselas?)

It is possible to
build a central entrance
gate into the angle of a building
as here. But is it likely?

38. Work in progress: a selection of sketch-book notes

at Ashland, Oregon; at Chichester in Sussex, and at many other places throughout the world.

Therefore since all this is undoubtedly the case, the question again arises: if the Globe is to be rebuilt, and since if it is to be the Globe in an historical sense it could not be rebuilt to serve as a theatre in the modern sense, what then could or should be the use of it?

I submit that its use should be considered under two separate but equal heads: it should be built (i) as an Exhibit; and (ii) as an Auditorium—which is not in modern terms the same thing as a theatre, though it may be used for one.

As an exhibit the Globe would certainly and above all be a unique attraction in its own right, an object of colourful interest which could confidently be expected to draw visitors from all over the world. It would, after all, be a building unlike any other in the world, and a theatre that has not been seen under the sun for over three hundred years. As part of its attraction there could be presented in it, perhaps three or four times a day at certain seasons, short demonstration performances of, let us say, half an hour's duration. These performances would show the typical uses of the stage and its effects under Jacobean conditions. The audience in the yard would stand. They would see Romeo at Juliet's window, the descent of a throne in glory from the Heavens, and Faustus being dragged down by devils into Hell. There would be perhaps a drum and trumpet entry to symbolize an army, and a battle of 'four or five most vile and ragged foils'. There would, of course, be Elizabethan music, played on the early type of instruments, and there would be a Presenter to introduce and explain the show. It hardly needs saying that a demonstration performance of this kind, perhaps more extended, would be of the greatest value to school audiences.

As a variant (or continuation) of the two uses just described, the Globe would house a theatre museum or exhibition, of which it would itself be the principal exhibit. (Ideally, it would be the centrepiece of a British Theatre Museum.) Thus visitors would go not only into the galleries but into the tiring-house also, where they would find the costumes, make-up, properties, prompt-books, and all the other gear of an Elizabethan player–company, laid out as if ready for a performance. It will of course be noted that none of these three uses would be effective unless the building were in fact a reconstruction in the fullest possible sense. In a 'modernized' Elizabethan, or 'Elizabethanized' modern theatre they would have no meaning nor any interest.

I come now to the Globe used as an auditorium. As in the case of the roof, certain modifications would have to be made for the sake of practicality. These modifications could be concealed, however. As an example, let us take the height of the stage, and its relation to the yard in which it stands. There is no question that it would be necessary for the yard to be seen normally clear of seats, as if for the standing audience of 'groundlings' around a high stage. But it might—indeed it very likely would—for some purposes be convenient and necessary to place seating in the yard, and for a seated audience the stage would then be too high. Therefore its height should be made adjustable. It could be made to sink mechanically to a lower level as and when required. The governing principle to be observed in dealing with modern additions and equipment is that as far as possible they should be hidden so as not to conflict with the historic appearance; but where that is not possible, as in the case of the roof, or with, say, the arrangements for stage lighting, these should be seen as modern fitments specially imported and applied to an old building which is not to be altered or damaged in any way: by implication, these fitments are to be removed when not needed, leaving the building unaltered, in its original state. That is certainly what would happen at the original Globe, if in fact that had been preserved and were to be used, as the Teatro Olimpico at Vicenza is used, for occasional festival performances.

With these adjustments, then, the Globe auditorium would be convertible for many different purposes, though always easily reconvertible to its true appearance as a Jacobean playhouse. In spite of a limited audience capacity it should during some part of the year present a season of Shakespearian or 'Jacobethan' plays, in the original manner. But at other times it would provide an excellent setting for concerts of chamber music; and it would be especially suitable as a locale for jazz, folk music, and pop concerts, the vernacular entertainments of our day which are surely an equivalent to those of the Elizabethan popular play-houses. On more formal occasions the building would be used for conferences, receptions, political or other gatherings, and for certain kinds of sporting events. In short it would be a public meeting place for all sorts of occasions. But it would not and probably should not be expected to meet the particular, sophisticated, versatile, and very expensive requirements of a modern professional theatre.

But ultimately its chief purpose and justification would be to exist as itself, the Globe, the restoration of Shakespeare's workshop, the cradle and school of the modern theatre, the physical representative of one of the greatest episodes in the history of the European culture. If it is true, as is not likely to be denied, that Shakespeare stands, alone of all British creative artists, in the great company of Bach, Beethoven, and Michelangelo, it is perhaps not too much to expect that somewhere in the world, and of course most properly in Britain, his theatre, at present the missing monument of the dramatic art, will be rebuilt. In the hope that it may one day be done I offer this book as a contribution and a beginning.